LIGHT IN

ARCHITECTURE

© 2007 Tectum Publishers
Godefriduskaai 22
Antwerp, Belgium
tel. +32 3 226 66 73
www.tectum.be
ISBN: 978-90-76886-45-9
WD: 2007/9021/10
(38)
Author: Mireia Vergés
Editor in chief: Inma Alavedra
Editor : Julie Meyers
Design: S. García
English translation: Heather Bagott

Editorial project:
Vertigo Publishers - UDYAT S.L.
Viladomat 158-160 int.
08015 Barcelona - Spain
Tel. +34 933 631 068
Fax. +34 934 522 544
www.vertigopublishers.com
info@vertigopublishers.com

Printed in UE by Ferré Olsina

LIGHT IN
ARCHITECTURE

TECTUM
PUBLISHERS

EXTERIOR LIGHTING 374

LIGHT IN
ARCHITECTURE

Light determines our perception of architecture. It enables us to appreciate the diverse qualities of the spaces: size, geometric shape, texture, colour... It is perhaps the element with the greatest influence over the atmosphere of a place. The correct illumination intensifies the poetic and emotional impact of a project.

This book provides a general insight into the world of lighting, natural as well as artificial, with examples of up to date projects which show the fascinating interaction between light and architecture. The first part deals with the lighting of buildings and interior spaces where the possibilities of manipulating light are practically endless. The second part studies the illumination of exteriors, in urban settings as well as in parks, gardens and landscapes.

Natural illumination has always played a central role in the history of architecture. Sunlight follows a daily cycle and is characterised by its constant variation. Its qualities vary over the day and also through the seasons. In Romanesque, Gothic and Baroque architecture, buildings were designed to be able to control and manipulate the qualities of natural light in order to enhance the shapes of the interior space of buildings and achieve the desired ambience. The type of openings, their size, location and orientation as well as the geometry and dimensions of the interiors are defining features. The material through which the light flows, the texture and colour of the surfaces with which it comes into contact, are also important points to consider. The designer should be well aware of the resources available with which to alter and improve the conditions of sunlight.

The basis for a suitable natural illumination is without doubt a good architectural project providing ventilation and light in all the rooms. Sunlight is the most economical and also the most beneficial for health and well-being. This said, an excess of natural light can cause annoyance and may not provide the right kind of illumination needed to carry out certain activities. There are ways to avoid undesirable effects, namely meshes, slats, filters, special glass... By being creative with the finishing of the surfaces and the magic of mirrors, an interior space can seem brighter. However, a good illumination project has to consider darkness and shadows as well as light. In the words of the Swiss architect Peter Zumthor, "How much light does man need, and how much darkness?" Both are of course necessary for the balance and well-being of people.

With regard to artificial lighting, these are times of great evolution, not only because of the constant technological advances but also in relation to its growing worth and importance in all kinds of projects. As already mentioned, in general, natural light has always formed part of the composition of architectural projects from the beginning of the planning process. Unfortunately, this cannot always be said for artificial lighting. For many years the study of the illumination of a building was limited to solving the functional and safety problems. The main aim was to guarantee sufficient levels of light to carry out any given activity without really taking other factors, such as psychological comfort and visual fatigue, into account. Fortunately the outlook is changing and there are a growing number of designers who understand the expressive possibilities of artificial light and its influence on people's moods. It has been a gradual process which many factors have influenced.

One of the principal factors is technological development with the arrival of more economical light sources with a greater chromatic reproduction capacity. There have also been advances in light modulation and regulation systems. Some specialists, as for example Kaoru Mende, believe that artificial light, like natural light, should be variable and dynamic and somehow show the passing of time. In a way, it should adapt itself to the rhythms of nature. This is made possible by programming scenes and incorporating IT into the illumination technology. Systems which interact with the surroundings, either by way of sensors, or by signals created by the users themselves, are also being developed. Other innovations worth mentioning are media facades which project dynamic images and illuminate the urban landscape.

Another factor which has influenced the growing importance of artificial lighting is the confirmation of the commercial, economic and environmental benefits gained by choosing the appropriate illumination. It has been demonstrated that illumination in the workplace can affect the performance and satisfaction levels of the workers. It can also represent the difference between the success and the failure of shops, hotels and restaurants. Who would not prefer to dine in a cosy candle lit restaurant, rather than one lit by cold intermittent fluorescents?

On another level, artistic creation has also influenced the way in which artificial light is used in architectural projects. In the decade of the seventies, artists such as Dan Flavin and James Turrell investigated at length the spectacular alterations in the perception of a space due to the presence of very simple luminous objects. The work of many lighting specialists is closely connected to the spirit of experimentation of these artists.

An illumination project can highlight the qualities of an architectural or interior design and also conceal the flaws of a project in the half-light. The growing complexity of the world of illumination has led to the demand for specialists with a thorough and up to date knowledge of lighting technology and of the existing innovation in the field of design. Ideally, architects and illumination specialists should work together from the outset so that they both have a full understanding of the overall aims of the project and the desired final ambience. In the majority of projects presented in this book, the effect of artificial light forms an integral part of the overall architectural concept.

Today, one of the principal aims of the illumination industry is the conservation of energy which means the investigation of new light sources will continue evolving. The control of light contamination is also a serious matter that needs improving. An understanding of the abuse of light at night and its negative effects on humans implies that one should act with moderation and respect in the lighting design for exterior spaces.

The selection of projects, grouped together by several characteristics of the lighting design that have been considered remarkable, is an attractive sample of the expressive possibilities of this field which is evermore sophisticated and demanding in the search for creating the desired ambience.

INTERIOR LIGHTING

In total darkness, the characteristics of a space cannot be appreciated. Light enables us to make out the dimensions, textures and colours of a place. The origins of architecture lie in the basic human need for protection against the elements such as overcoming extreme heat or cold, rain, sun or excessive light, which can interfere with everyday tasks. The illumination in any closed or partly closed space is what we call interior light. Natural light can only be controlled up to a certain point given its free and changeable nature. It can vary according to the time of day, the season, the levels of humidity or the colour of the clouds.

The same geometric space can assume a different appearance depending on the illumination. Direct midday sunlight with its resultant sharp contrasts gives a different feel to a space, as does the whitish diffused light of the northern countries. Light plays a large part in the perception of architecture. This especially affects the relationship between the interior and the exterior spaces, the degree of connection between them, and the importance of the exterior landscape in the rooms. In areas with intense bright light, such as the Mediterranean and Mexico, jalousies, porches, and arched patios are often used as spaces which create a transition between the exterior and domestic interior. In other places, such as England or the Netherlands, the interiors are opened up to the outside world with large windows and glass roofs through which the sky can be observed. The enormous glass skyscrapers of the high-tech architecture can be better understood knowing about this type of Anglo-Saxon architectural tradition.

The natural light usually flows into an interior space through openings in its facades (windows and doors) or in its roofs (zenithal light). These elements can be used to create an infinite number of effects. Today, large glass windows can be manufactured to minimize the division between exterior and interior, while maintaining optimal temperatures. The patio is another element that guarantees maximum illumination and ventilation in the interior of buildings, an effective solution which consists of a limited lateral space with an open superior plane. Here the windows overlook a designed space, not a natural or artificial landscape.

As Josep Quetglas wrote... "light is an interior phenomenon". It is inside where light can be observed, where it projects itself onto surfaces whose qualities, intensity and colours are thus brought into view. Shadows, however, are more distinguishable on the exterior.

The architectural project involves choosing the position, the size and shape of the spaces through which the natural light will flow. Architecture, "the wise game, correct and magnificent of assembled volumes in the light" as Le Corbusier said, reaches its greater expression when light meets form.

The advances in the technology of artificial light over the last century have enabled the architectural game of light and spaces to be played at all hours of the day and night.

NATURAL LIGHTING

NATURAL LIGHTING

Natural light is considered the one which comes from the sun. The nature of light has been discussed for centuries. Life would be unthinkable without light. However, it is also true that light has been and always will be a fascinating and mysterious element.

In the 17th century, Isaac Newton exposed his corpuscular theory of light. After several experiments with prisms, Newton reached the conclusion that white light was made from all the colours of the rainbow. His corpuscular theory explains that the light is made up of luminous "bodies or particles" which are spread in straight lines. These bodies can pass through transparent materials and are reflected by opaque materials.

A short time after (around 1678), Christian Huygens, opposing Newton's theory, defined light as a movement of waves, in which luminous waves spread through an invisible and insubstantial matter called ether. Over the following centuries, many studied the oscillations of the waves of light in space. In 1887 Heinrich Hertz discovered the photoelectric phenomenon which involves the spontaneous emission of electrons in a conductor when light is projected. Albert Einstein explained this in 1905, highlighting the emission of luminous energy by photons and the quantum nature of light.

Today light is considered to have a dual wave/particle nature which explains in a different way the phenomenon of its propagation (wavy nature) and the effects of the interaction of light with material (corpuscular nature).

Visible light is a kind of electromagnetic radiation emitted on a set wavelength, between 380 and 760 nanometres. The electromagnetic spectrum corresponds to a narrow strip situated between the infrared waves (of longer wavelength) and the ultraviolet waves (of shorter wavelength). Within the band of visible light, there are radiations of every colour of the rainbow, going from red (on the infrared radiation side) to violet (alongside the ultraviolet rays). The white light appears when all the wavelengths of the visible spectrum are present in identical intensity and proportions.

Light is projected onto objects whose surfaces absorb or reflect the radiations of different frequencies of the visible spectrum. The colour of an object will depend on the characteristics of the light projected onto it and on the radiations that the material reflects. In this way, a blue object illuminated with white light reflects mainly the radiations which correspond to the blue strip of the spectrum and absorbs the rest. That the human eye is sensible to this phenomenon enables us to perceive the world as we know it.

TRANSPARENCY

The architectural project, in addition to defining the situation, orientation, geometry and size of the openings or windows, also determines the material through which the natural light is transmitted. This material affects the light's characteristics, and can be transparent, translucent or opaque, and it can also vary depending on the circumstances.

The Webster dictionary defines the adjective transparent as – "having the property of transmitting light without appreciable scattering so that bodies lying beyond are seen clearly." It is also said to be "clear, evident, and understood without any doubt or ambiguity." A transparent object does not distort the vision of that which is on the other side.

In air nearly all rays are transmitted without significant changes in direction or chromatics. In other instances, only light of a specific wavelength is transmitted without changes, which is the case in the coloured crystal. The transparency of an object is calculated by its transmittance, or the percentage of light intensity that goes through it.

Transparent surfaces scarcely modify the qualities of the light that goes through them. If they receive direct and intense light, the result is an unfiltered illumination which maintains its contrast with well defined projected shadows.

The most common transparent materials in architecture are glass (with its ever growing product range) and certain plastics, such as methacrylate.

In architecture, the use of transparent surfaces manages to unite visually the exterior and the interior, creating spatial continuity. It enables views and landscapes to be enjoyed from inside the buildings. The characteristics of the openings will influence the vision of the outdoor landscape. For example, a small window can frame a certain detail of the location, concealing the chaotic surroundings.

The modern architecture movement pursued this effect of spatial continuity between interior and exterior, resulting in the extensive usage of glass. Mies van der Rohe's Farnsworth house (1949-1951) is a paradigm of this tendency – a glass box in the middle of the Illinois forest which proved a misfortune for the owner, Miss Farnsworth. It is said that the famous architect seduced his client into developing such an innovative and radical project. Once the work and the probable romance had ended, the proprietor felt unable to live with so little privacy and under the extreme climatic conditions that the glass house presented and initiated a legal battle. Finally, the architect won the trial and the client sold the house. It is true that the greenhouse effect is one of the main problems in using large panes of glass and therefore a correct orientation is essential. The ideal orientation is north. Large panes of glass must provide thermal and acoustic insulation and must be protected to prevent excessive external light and heat.

During the day, sunlight illuminates the interior of buildings. At night, the opposite phenomenon occurs, and it is the artificial light which is projected out onto the urban space through the facade. This is a desired effect in contemporary architecture, particularly in public buildings, such as the New Trade Fair Milano or the Villa Moda Department Store.

TRANSPARENCY

HOUSE IN HIGHGATE

Architect: Eldridge Smerin Architects
Location: London, UK
Year: 2001
Sqm: 600

Although many of the rooms within the house are lit from a grid of carefully positioned flush mounted spotlights, the new studio space, that sits on top of the house and helps give it its distinctive appearance, has a particular lighting strategy to reinforce that of the architecture. The entire ceiling surface is lit by linear fluorescent uplighters concealed at the head of a series of upstand walls that frame the staircase to below and a small kitchenette and WC. The wash of light on the ceiling helps accentuate the floating quality of the ceiling as it rakes gently up either side. The colour of the light can be alterered for particular occasions by the addition of coloured gels on the light fittings.

To the rear a strip of linear flourescent downlighters in a pocket next to the glazing helps light the balcony area beyond. To the front the frame-less glass panels and roof of the studio element have a translucent film applied below head height which turns the glass into a diffuse glowing surface when seen from the street in the evening. In contrast, during the day it disappears from view and becomes part of the sky behind.

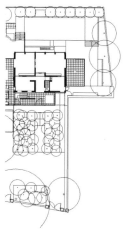

NEW TRADE FAIR MILANO

Architect: Massimiliano Fuksas
Location: Milano, Italy
Year: 2005
Sqm: 1 000 000

The New Trade Fair is an important project for the region of Milan. Its dimensions make it one of the largest buildings in Europe. It is part of the wide structure of suburban space which is located in the outskirts of the city. This space wants to become "geography" and wants to be "landscape".

The project is characterized by a central axis. The transparent covering of the axis modifies space and represents the vision of continuity. The service centre, offices and exhibition areas are scattered within the vast site area.

The pavilions are situated on both sides of the axis. Their reflective facades coated with steel panels mirror the image of people walking. The main entrances to the complex are sculpturally designed to the two ends of the path. The architecture can be described as "contaminated" art: it survives by relying on other "universes." It controls movement and changes; it tries to represent what's going on. Architecture is not only inspired by architecture, but tends to relate to every single person. In a situation with very few visions for the future, this projects creates dynamic sceneries. Obviously there is a demand for architecture, a demand for emotion.

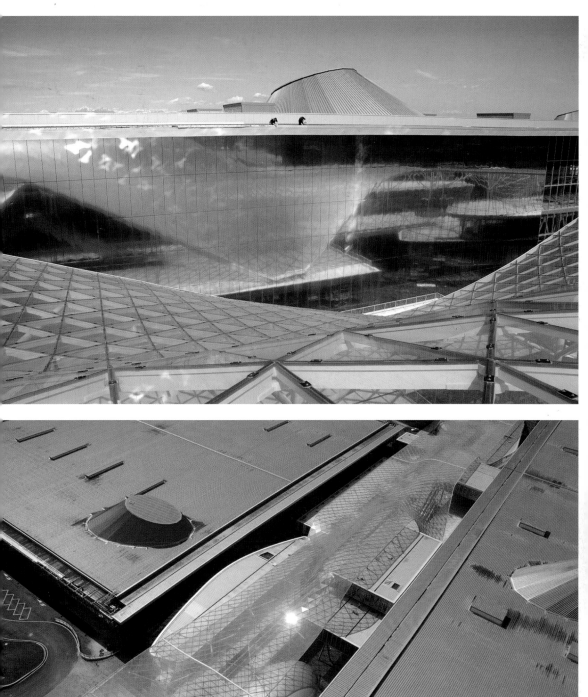

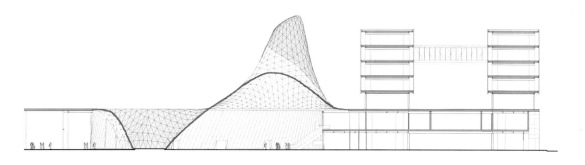

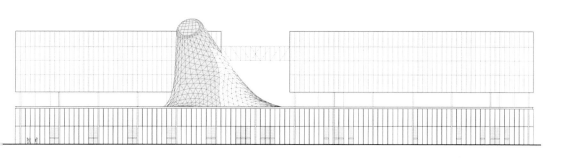

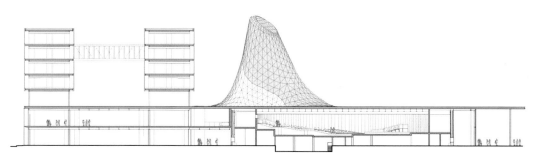

TRANSPARENCY

VILLA MODA

Architect: Eldridge Smerin Architects
Location: Kuwait City, Kuwait
Year: 2002
Sqm: 5000

Unlike the conventional department store, which tends to be a closed box, the concept for Villa Moda was to allow views out across the harbour to the city skyline and beyond. This also allowed much of the internal lighting to be from daylight through the glass curtain walling that wraps the building and a series of large glazed openings in the roof. To deal with the intense sunlight of a Middle Eastern summer each rooflight has a diffuser created from dozens of folded polycarbonate sections butted together.

To light the store at night, a grid of adjustable downlighters covers the ceiling, which is a continuous white plane. Recessed track lighting also allows areas of the floors to be lit in various ways to suit the changing displays. With the store open late into the evening to enable its clients to avoid the worst of the daytime heat in the summer months, external lighting was of equal importance. Eldridge Smerin surrounded the entire building with a 'forest' of steel masts which are the same height as the building. Each mast is topped by an LED light fitting which helps create a halo of light around the building and identifies it from afar. When the sun is out the masts also create a rippling field of shadows that echo the graphic pattern on the stores distinctive bags.

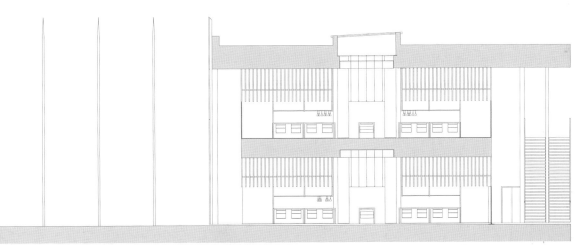

TRANSLUCENCE

When a material allows light to flow through it, but not vision, it is called translucent. The Webster dictionary defines this adjective as "having the property of transmitting and diffusing light so that objects beyond cannot be seen clearly". The view through a translucent body insinuates what is behind in a partial, unclear manner. In translucent bodies the direction of the rays which are transmitted is modified slightly, and absorption as well as reflection of some of the radiation occurs. This produces a diffuse, soft light with hardly any contrast between light and dark. The difference between the brightest and the darkest areas will be gradual, and a better colour perception of the intermediate tones of the illuminated objects is achieved.

The light which is transmitted through a translucent surface is ambiguous and mysterious as its source is not easily seen. The spaces that have this type of illumination normally conceal the exterior view, which enhances the sensation of seclusion. The abstract quality of this light favours concentration. The isolation from exterior features makes these spaces appropriate for contemplation and prayer. As early as in Romanesque architecture, alabaster stone was used to cover the openings, bringing spirituality and serenity to the interiors of churches. This sacred light is common in some of today's new contemporary temples, which are great museums and cultural centres.

Translucent materials do not allow clear vision through them, as they only provide blurred silhouettes. Looking through the material towards the brighter side, shapes can be made out, while the other way around it is impossible to see anything. An exterior opening of translucent glass guarantees privacy during the day when the exterior light is more intense. At night, views of the interior will remain protected whereas the interior lights are noticeable from the exterior. The silhouettes of people who move close to the window may also be seen. This type of material used along the facade is converted into large diffusers of light which illuminate the urban space. A spectacular example is the Department Store Omega in Czech Republic and the Limoges Concert Hall in France. These buildings of intriguing poetry are most expressive at night, when they become beautiful urban luminaries.

Glass is one of the principal materials when constructing translucent elements. They can be built using acid treated glass, laminated glass, glass with a vinyl coating, u-glass, and also different types of glass blocks, such as glass bricks. Plastics such as polycarbonate or methacrylate are also very common in the construction of translucent surfaces and are lighter and more thermally insulating than glass.

There have been great advances in investigation into plastic materials in recent years. Today, one of the most innovative materials is translucent cement with fibre optics, which in addition to conserving the mechanical properties of cement, allows light to pass through them, like alabaster and other types of stone.

TRANSLUCENCE

DEPARTMENT STORE OMEGA

Architect: Kuba & Pilar Architekti - Ladislav Kuba, Tomáš Pilar
Location: Brno, Czech Republic
Year: 2005
Sqm: 2 904 + 87 Atrium

The site allocated for the building of Department Store Omega is situated at the Svobody sq. in Brno. The site forms part of a city block containing many significant buildings interweaved with inner passages.

The architectural design of the main facade oriented towards the Svobody square works with exact geometric articulation of the mass in delimited frame of frontage. A plane of structurally hanged translucent milk glass within the facade is perforated by dark metal boxes, providing both depth along with window openings from floor to floor. A key element of the design is the contrast of these materials with the vertical composition of the window openings. The luminance of the milk glass during the night gives the building another dimension.

The facade of the building comprises a structural glazing system with an outer pane of toughened glass, laminated to an inner pane of partially toughened clear glass through an opaque interlayer. This glazing, hung from pre-cast cantilevered ceiling slabs, forms part of a double facade system and hangs outside an inner masonry structure. Fixings for the glazing are made only to the inner skin giving a frameless effect when viewed from the outside. Openings within the masonry structure are formed by double glazed window units. Aluminium sheets are folded and welded to form the reveals, with service hatches provided to access the ventilated service cavity with lighting behind.

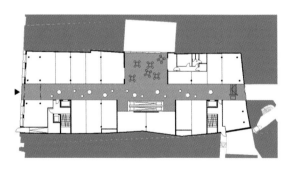

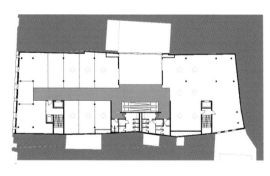

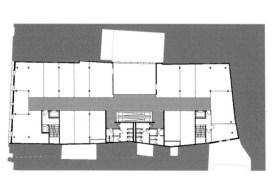

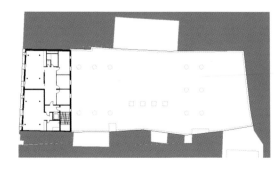

he opaque part of the facade is lit from a ventilated cavity. The laminating interlayer of the glass provides distribu-
on of the light from linear sources placed at the floor slabs of the cavity. The colour of the light is composed of the
olour of the light sources, the colour of the cover's top foil and the colour of the glass interlayer.

TRANSLUCENCE

LIMOGES CONCERT HALL

Architects: Bernard Tschumi Architects
Location: Limoges, France
Year: 2007
Sqm: 850

The Concert Hall in Limoges, located in the center of France, returns to the general envelope concept already explored in Rouen but transforms it through a new material strategy. In Rouen, the outer envelope was made of steel and the inner envelope of exposed concrete. In Limoges, the outer envelope is made of wood arcs and translucent rigid polycarbonate sheets and the inner envelope of wood.

The use of wood was suggested by the location of the hall, in a clearing within a large forest surrounded by trees over 200 years old. In addition, the soft translucency of the polycarbonate complemented the wooden frame by allowing light to filter in and out of the building. The strategy establishes reciprocity between concept and context.

Limoges's detached and fragmented envelope opens in two directions, towards both the forest and the road. Between the two envelopes are the movement vectors: two ramps, one extending downward toward the lower tiers of the auditorium, and the other upward toward the upper tiers.

Much of the material treatment is determined by energy conservation and sustainability considerations. The highest portion of the facade has a pixelated design silk-screened directly on the shell for additional solar protection.

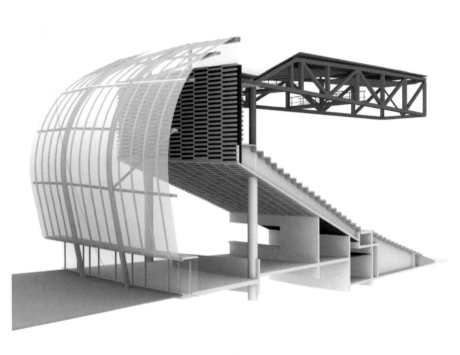

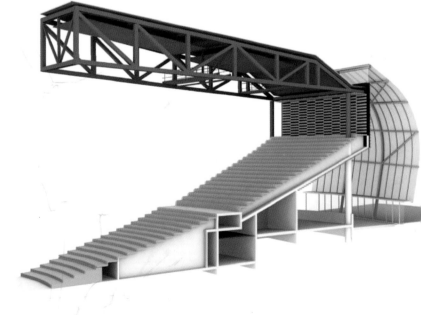

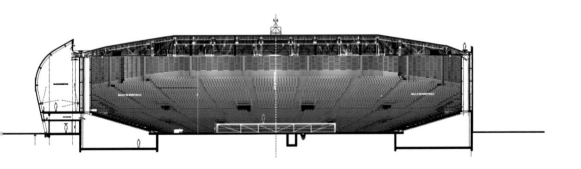

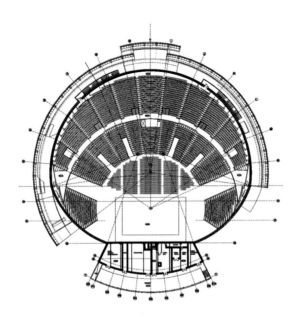

TRANSLUCENCE

THE CHRIST PAVILION, EXPO 2000 AND VOLKENRODA MONASTERY

Architect: GMG Architekten
Location: Hanover, Germany
Year: 2000
Sqm: 18 548

The Pavilion of Christian Religions, a combined contribution of the Catholic and Protestant Churches for the EXPO 2000, is intended to be a contemplative counterpart to the vanity fair with architectural highlights: simple in structure, reduced to a few materials, precise in detail and unmistakable in its appearance and spatial atmosphere. The architecture of the Pavilion is restricted to the clear presentation of the modular construction and its details. The modest and simple choice of materials, steel, glass, gravel and water, are "decorated" with the addition of one large tree.

The spatial atmosphere of all areas is created by a modulation of light. The "Christ Hall" receives light from top-lights centrally located above the column heads, emphasizing the vertical quality of the slender columns. The surrounding surfaces of thinly cut marble form a light-transmissive envelope, its lively colours creating a spatial atmosphere. In contrast, the lighting emphasis in the "crypt" is solemn; thin light slots along the column axis and a surrounding strip of light in the floor create a focus which emphasizes the character of concrete and renders a mystical intensity through the effects of shadows.

The surrounding "cloister" is equipped with a double glass facade, used as large-scale showcases. The space between is filled with various materials from nature and technology as part of the overall presentation. Depending on the respective content, the glass walls are more or less translucent or partially transparent. The whole complex was dismantled after the EXPO in Hanover and re-erected in a modified form in the Cistercian Monastery in Volkenroda, Thüringen in 2001.

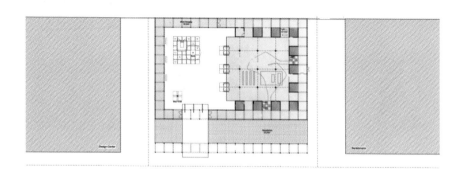

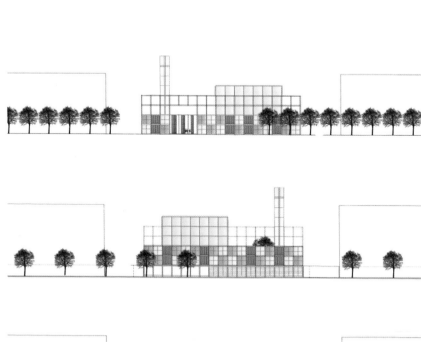

JALOUSIES
AND LATTICES

Depending on the place, season and time of day, direct solar radiation can become a nuisance. Excessive light is blinding and can be a nuisance for certain activities which require concentration. Prolonged exposure can be tiring and uncomfortable. In hot countries, the traditional architecture has striven to overcome this problem by developing complex systems to provide protection from the sun – porches, gazebos, jalousies, folding slat openings, blinds. As well as being very efficient in controlling solar rays, these also provide coolness in the summer months, a good way of saving energy from air condition systems.

These solar protection systems can be split into two groups: those which are on the horizontal, such as pergolas, gazebos, arbours, porches and brise-soleils, and those which are on the vertical, or in front of facades and windows.

Lattices and gazebos are often found in parks and other public spaces. Markets and winding streets covered with roofs made from reeds are typical in cities of Arab tradition. The shadows created by these elements are aesthetically very pleasing, leaving the streets in a kind of soft half-light, bathed in a delicate zenithal illumination. Architecture is not only able to manipulate light, but it can also create shadows. A good example of this can be found in the work of artist Cristina Iglesias whose lattice installations enhance the emotion of these spaces defined by light, not walls.

Besides their aesthetic qualities, shaded spaces are very practical in hot climates. Not only do they protect from the suns rays, but in urban or semi urban zones they give greater intimacy to corners of patios and gardens, such as dining or lounge areas. Another plus is that they are able to conceal undesirable views. For example, in Barcelona, some bars and hotels use pergolas to conceal chaotic and untidy spaces in patios, creating more appealing, controlled and comfortable exterior areas. Gazebos with awnings or those with plant elements are especially advisable because they provide protection from excessive heat and light in summer but allow the sun rays in winter, when they are very pleasant.

The vertical elements of solar protection, such as blinds or slats are very desirable in southern climates, especially those with south or east facing openings (in the northern hemisphere). As well as providing great savings in air conditioning (even more so if they are situated on the exterior part of the facade), they provide adequate lighting inside. Most importantly, they prevent overwhelming light by filtering the light and diffusing it evenly around the space. Some slat systems modify the direction of the rays, causing them to be reflected on the ceiling for example, thus creating an additional indirect illumination.

Today there are also many types of glass which can be used as protection against excessive radiations, such as reflective glass, which also filters light, low emissivity glass, and large windows with vinyl coatings. These elements can form true eye catching features on the facades.

Since the nineties, as much for environmental reasons as for aesthetic trends, the study of the "skin" of buildings has been pushed to the forefront of contemporary architecture, with very interesting work being carried out.

LOUIS VUITTON OMOTESANDO

Architect: Jun Aoki & Associates
Interior design: Eric Carlson & David Mac Nulty
Location: Shibuya-ku, Tokyo
Year: 2002
Sqm: 512

Louis Vuitton Omotesando is a store building 25.5 meters wide, 20.8 meters deep and 31.9 meters high, made up of rectangular parallel-piped units stacked in an irregular pile. The structure, located in interstitial spaces 30 centimeters deep and 37 centimeters high between the rectangular parallel-piped units, is a non-uniform cage with several vertically aligned columns. The columns and beams are all made from wide-flange steel 20 centimeters by 20 centimeters in cross-sections.

The exterior finish consists of two types of metal mesh, polished stainless panels and two layers of glass ornamented with patterns.

LV Hall on the seventh floor has a triple-height ceiling and is wrapped in a three-layered screen of metal mesh, glass and white lace embroidered with white ribbons.

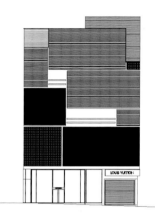

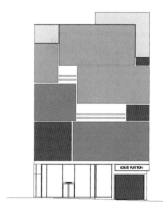

JALOUSIES AND LATTICES

PARIS OFFICES

Architect: Francisco José Mangado Beloqui
Location: Paris, France
Year: under construction
Sqm: 45 000

The city of Paris has almost exhausted the possiblity of building downtown. For this reason, the superstores that stem from the railway coverings have transformed into fixed objectives. In this case they will try to occupy, with basic uses as offices and stores, the space that would result from the area situated between the railways of Saint Lazare and the Plaza de Europa.

In the proposal, urban and infrastructural nature go hand in hand. The importance of structure and mechanics of the operation makes us appreciate the resulting awe-inspiring spaces in the 19 large stations. A space of this nature would be capable of uniting the same power and magnificence necessary to the success of the urban dimenson. This idea supports the proposal of a large metalic structure covered in aluminum that shapes the great evolvement of the entire intervention and that constitutes the same urban image.

The external structure acts at the same time like a brise-soleil, which redirects light and defines shades in the interior.

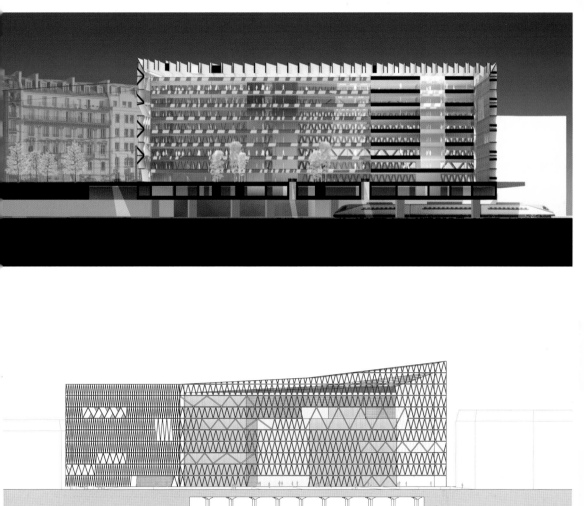

JALOUSIES AND LATTICES

SADO BOTTLING FACTORY NISACO

Architect: Norihiko Dan
Location: Niigata Prefecture. Niigata, Japan
Year: 2005
Sqm: 1 012

Located on Sado Island near the ocean, this factory is a facility for bottling water that contains minerals extracted from deep sea water.

In consideration of the salt air, the structure of the main building comprises a vault roof made of short pieces of laminated timber supported by a row of wooden louver columns. The louver columns are set at a 45 degree angle to gather morning sunlight from the east and prevent glare from the setting sun in the west.

From the inside, the facade also serves as a large window that absorbs the changes in light brought by the sun's progression and allows a dialogue with the tranquil rural scenery outside.

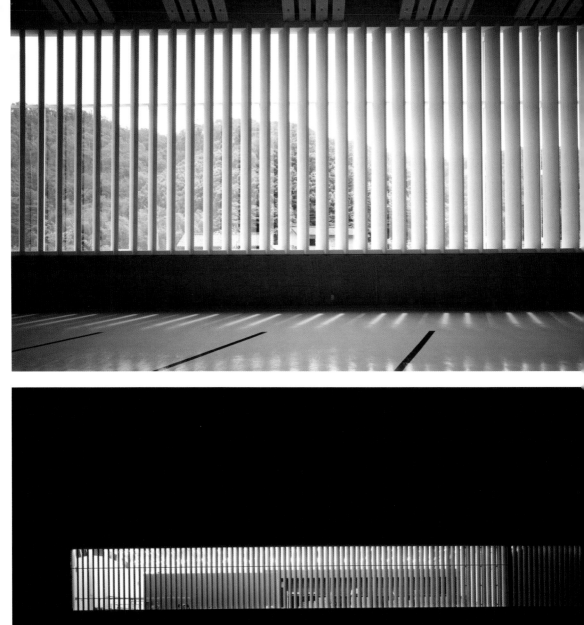

In order to make the factory open to the surrounding environment, the long facade extending horizontally functions as a screen that affords views, both day and night, of the factory interior from the road - views that change depending on the observer's perspective.

ZENITH LIGHT AND OCULUS

When natural light flows into a space from above, usually through skylights, it is known as zenithal light. These openings absorb more radiations over the course of a day than a window of the same size because of their position. Their design and construction need careful thought in hot climates and should take the following into consideration: static capacity, thermic and acoustic protection, weather proofing, the prevention of breakage, controlling possible condensation, the mechanic capability (which should be enough to withstand wind and the weight of snow) and of course, the quality of light. There are, however, other ways to illuminate with zenithal light without skylights. In buildings with double height spaces or complex sections, light may enter through vertical openings from upper levels, illuminating the levels that are below. In large industrial warehouses, trade fair areas, markets, and so on, awnings of different heights enable sizeable areas to be illuminated in various ways and with great formal expressivity.

The architect Louis Kahn said that all spaces need natural light. In interior rooms, zenithal illumination is often the best way to achieve it. This type of light gives a certain atmosphere. Generally, it creates introverted ambiences, in which the public facade of the building is a world away from the interior qualities. Zenithal light is theatrical and easy to manipulate. Often, the light source is concealed thus enhancing its dramatic and mysterious character. This was a very popular effect in the Baroque architecture with impressive examples such as la Capilla Cornaro in Santa Maria Della Vittoria (Roma) by Gian Lorenzo Bernini. Inside the chapel, which holds the famous sculpture The Ecstasy of Santa Teresa, also by Bernini, the zenithal light serves as metaphor for the spiritual illumination of the Saint. Zenithal light is commonplace in churches and temples, enhancing elaborate compositions of volume, as seen in Hagia Sophia in Istanbul, whose spatial richness comes to life due to the diverse entries of light into the domes.

When the skylight is circular and situated at the highest point of a dome, it is called an oculus. This is a noun which originates from the Latin oculus, meaning eye. Perhaps it refers to the place through which the gods can watch over their followers. The most important oculus in the history of architecture is, without a doubt, the one in the Pantheon in Rome - a roman temple with a circular plan which has been a Christian church since the 7th century. As in other examples, there is nothing in the hermetic exterior facade which would suggest such an impressive interior. Inside there is a large 43 meter dome, illuminated by the rays which enter through a central oculus 9 meters in diameter. The oculus is uncovered so the rain and snow can also get in. Originally, the coffering of the dome was painted in blue and decorated with stars. The sun's rays are the highlight of the space and illuminate the surface of the dome recreating the stars' movement in the cosmos. This reference to the firmament is present in many other constructions illuminated by zenithal light, such as the Arab baths, libraries and even sports stadiums, such as the Palace of Sports in Rome built in 1958-60 by Pier Luigi Nervi. Light can obtain surprising effects when it is projected with a clear intention. Zenithal light, when depth and emotion are used, brings great expressivity and poetry to architecture.

ZENITH LIGHT AND OCULUS

THE TAICHUNG
METROPOLITAN OPERA HOUSE

Architect: Zaha Hadid with Patrik Schumacher

Location: Taichung, Taiwan

Year: not realized yet

Sqm: 28 000

The Taichung Metropolitan Opera House sets out to give the city of Taichung, Taiwan an exciting and new cultural venue in the city's new Civic District. The scheme comprises an opera with a 2009 seat Grand Auditorium, an 800 seat drama theatre and a 200 seat black box theatre, as well as artists' and crafts workshops and retail shops. A restaurant, gift shop, café and audience care facility are also included in the programme.

The majority of the programme will be situated in the main part of the building on the larger of the two site parcels. All three auditoriums, their associated facilities and the Cultural Plaza will constitute these programmes. The main entrance to the opera house is aligned with the cultural axis, facing southeast towards the intersection of the two axes. Leading up to this entrance is a large entrance ramp that swoops around the side of the building, taking people up from the southern edge of the site where the car and bus drop-off is located. A secondary entrance is situated on the northwest side of the building, also directly aligned with the cultural axis, to allow a flow to pass through the building. This is connected to the street level via a set of stairs and a ramp that wraps along the west side of the building. To the north of the site is the Shin Kong Mitsukoshi department store.

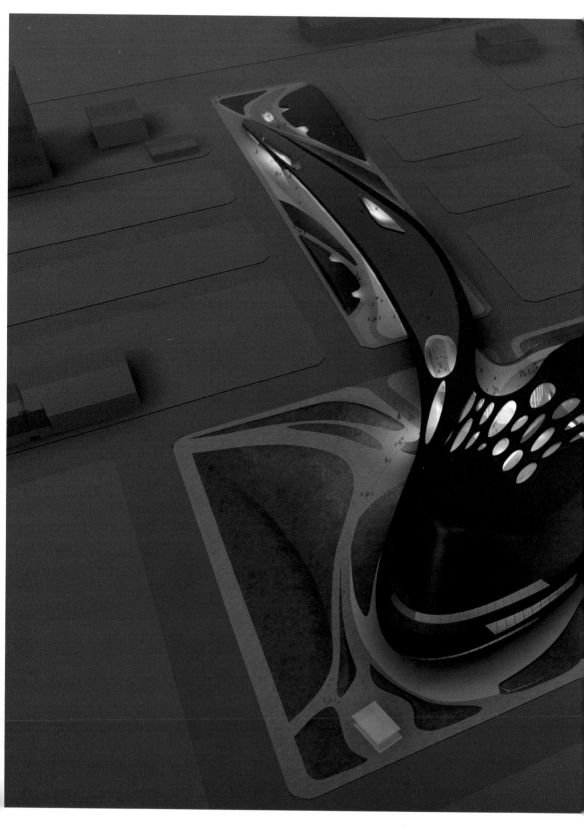

ZENITH LIGHT AND OCULUS

ENLARGEMENT OF THE KASTNER AND OHLER HEADQUARTERS

Architect: Nieto Sobejano Arquitectos, S.L.

Location: Graz, Austria

Year: under construction - 2008

Sqm: 5 000

The picturesque medieval rooftops of the historic centre of Graz have earned the town World Heritage value. The buildings of Kastner & Öhler have gradually taken over a large block near the town square since they built their headquarters there at the start of the 20th century.

The project is based on geometric law. Geometry has often been considered a limitation to formal liberty; however, it is the irregularity of the different buildings themselves, which make up the K&Ö headquarters, that has led to the creation of a pattern of rooftops which unify the complex.

In harmony with the slanting rooftops of the old city, a large folded plane rises and descends creating a series of dramatic skylights which generate different variations depending on the spaces included in their interior. Two new vertical nuclei – which run along all the floors – show the points where the skylights are the highest, letting in natural light along the whole length of the building, reminiscent of the large stairs housed within the primitive commercial buildings. Three terraces are created by the folds in the roof. The largest one serves as a cafe-restaurant with views over the magnificent rooftop scenery and the Schlossberg mountain. The different spaces in the program fit into the outline of the structure in line with the general geometric law.

A new landscape of rooftops is shown as a clear and precise changing volume in harmony with the irregular style of the existing rooftops.

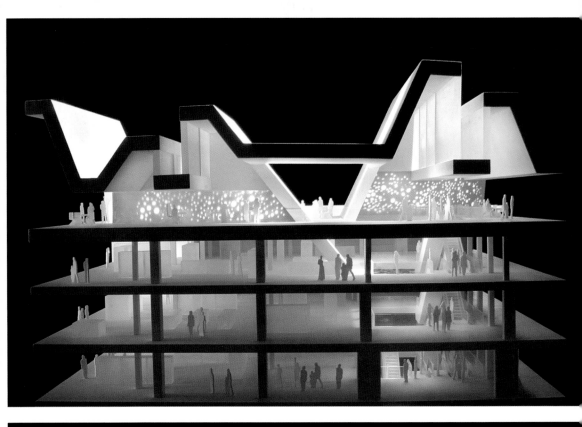
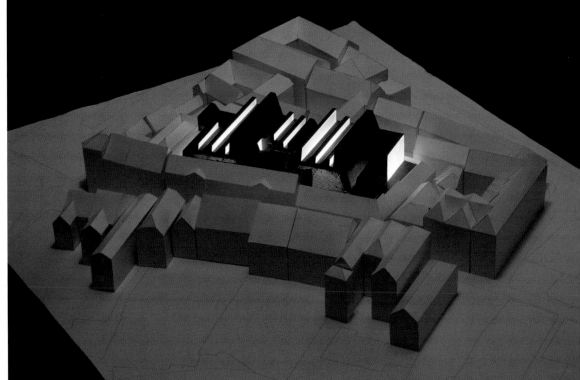

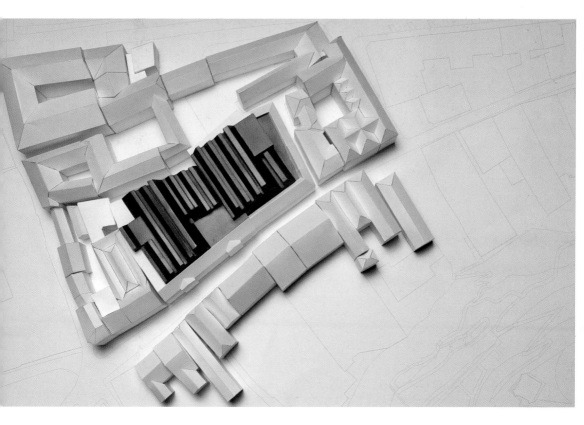

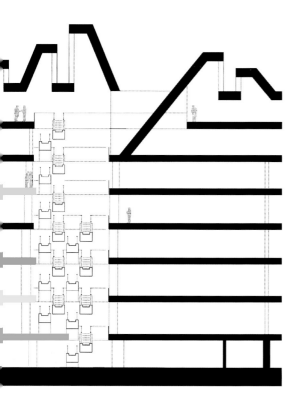

In the medieval and renaissance style architecture of the centre of Graz the new rooftops of the K&Ö headquarters rise up proudly and clearly, sketching a new profile, a geometric law or system which blends into the silhouette of a town whose greatest identity resides in its historic memory.

ZENITH LIGHT AND OCULUS

BALUARTE AUDITORIO Y PALACIO DE CONGRESOS DE NAVARRA

Architect: Mangado y Asociados
Location: Pamplona, Spain
Year: 2003
Sqm: 63 000

The most important project regards the final quantity and quality achieved in the recent history of Navarra, situated over what once was Ciudadela, a transitional area between the historic downtown and the urban expansions. The entire proposal turns the lathe into a fundamental idea, that is the resignation of the autonomous architectural project, proposing in its place a set, clear urban vocation.

Lighting always has a great worth when we talk about architecture. This project obtains an extraordinary importance that requires us to dedicate special care to the study and design of the illumination. Such effects have been applied to models and information programmes that we have been permitted to analyze the spacial incidence and the effects produced by the distinct types of light, simultaneously becoming the design prototype. Additionally, specific pieces for the building engage us to critically think about the illumination of the building.

the case of the exterior lighting, it gives the maximum character to buildings by manipulating the manner of
umination similar to a backdrop for the city, reflecting its levels according to distinct intensities that function with
e position of each volume. Also the wood, by means of the light reflection of the built-in focal points in the ceiling,
ill contribute to emphasise the reflection of the lights that simultaneously helps the illumination.

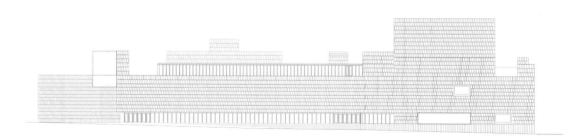

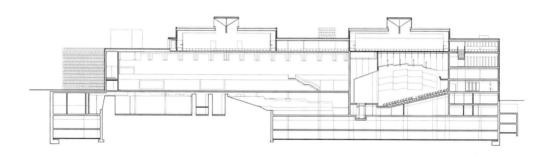

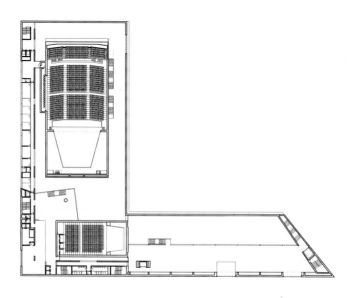

MIRRORS AND REFLECTION

Often, in architecture and interior design, the light we perceive is reflected. Optical reflection is the physical effect produced when a light wave changes its direction upon hitting a surface. Part of the radiation is reflected and returns to its source and part of it is absorbed. The percentage of each depends on the reflectance rate of the object.

To illuminate a certain space, it is important to know the reflectance factor of the surfaces that limit it. With the same intensity of light, a white plastered room is a great deal brighter than the same place covered with black velvet curtains. Reflection may be specular (that is, mirror-like) or diffuse (when the energy is retained, not the image). This is determined by the colour, roughness and structure of the reflective surface. On rough materials, the reflected waves bounce off in all directions due to the irregularities of the surface. In elements with completely smooth surfaces, like mirrors and ponds, the rays of light change their direction in a uniform manner, thus the waves remain parallel and the angle of reflection is the same as the angle of incidence.

The capability to redirect light through mirrors and specular materials offers great possibilities. This enables light to be channelled to places it does not reach naturally. Heliostats are mirrors designed to capture sunlight over the course of a day, concentrating the rays in a uniform direction. They redirect light to the lower levels of a ground floor courtyard or even illuminate an alpine retreat during the winter months – which is just what happens in the town of Viganella. There are also panels that are designed specifically to redirect the light, normally using double glass with reflecting elements inside the air chamber, like "Köster Sheets". These structures are oriented so that they protect from excessive sunlight in summer and reflect some of the light onto the ceiling giving a more even lighting. Another useful method to bring light into a dull space is using light wells or anidolic systems, which work like chimneys of light. These use mirrors to channel light by concentrating light towards interior rooms – usually basements or box rooms. Generally, they are north facing and by concentrating the light, the size of the opening outside is a third of that required by the traditional skylights.

As well as their ability to increase the general level of illumination, mirrors and other reflective surfaces may also modify the perception of the characteristics and dimensions of a space. Used correctly these elements can create spectacular effects in interior design. They are ideal for giving a greater sense of space in narrow and small rooms. They are commonplace in domestic, commercial and restaurant settings. Mirrors may also serve to redirect the sight towards a more pleasing view and also to control visually a space.

The mirror is to some extent an illusionist and a rather deceptive object, traditionally stirring feelings of distrust both in literature and architecture (probably puritan or of a purist nature). There are countless works which enhance its magical and sometimes disturbing qualities. In fairy stories and throughout tradition they appear as elements which connect parallel worlds, such as in *Through the Looking Glass* by Lewis Carrol. They are also linked to clairvoyance and wisdom, which is the case in the story of Sleeping Beauty and in Chaucer's *Canterbury Tales*. Their ability to catch souls and the fact that they cast no reflection of vampires is also common folklore. The use of mirrors in a space must be carefully studied to avoid feelings of disorientation and discomfort. Mirrors are infallible weapons for those who use them in the fields of architecture and interior design thanks to their enormous ability to manipulate and play with light and space.

MIRRORS AND REFLECTION

MIX RESTAURANT

Architect: Patrick Jouin and L'Observatoire
Location: Las Vegas, USA
Year: 2004
Sqm: 800

With panoramic views overlooking the Strip, MIX lives up to Las Vegas' reputation for extravagance with its menu signed by Alain Ducasse and the interior design entirely conceived and created by Patrick Jouin. Enchantment, glamour and humour are the main ingredients in this stunning cocktail.

Designer Patrick Jouin displays his talent with a modernist flair in a sumptuous, almost phantasmagorical setting featuring luxurious interiors highlighted by elegant details. It is a unique, ambitious, mind-boggling project that could only be spawned by a town like Las Vegas.

To begin with, MIX combines two very different atmospheres: the deep, sexy, entrancing red in the interior of the bar, and the purity of whiteness, translucent, in suspension and as airy as the skies, in the restaurant. It is a dramatic setting that provides unity of place, allowing you to move from the burning heart of the earth into a celestial cloud of water.

Created ex nihilo out of a completely empty "set," MIX now glows with a thousand nocturnal lights, just like the glass walls of the edifice which, like a two-way mirror that turns to gold after sunset, reflects the city as a backdrop while projecting the design of this restaurant, lounge and club over Las Vegas.

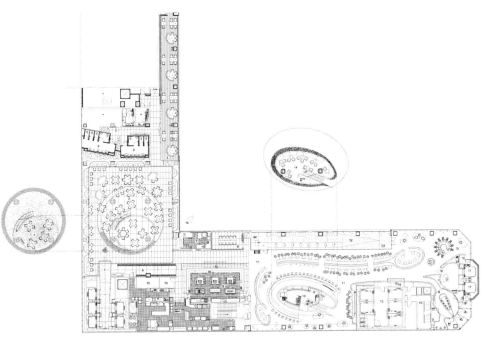

MIRRORS AND REFLECTION

HYDRAPIER

Architect: Asymptote

Location: Haarlemmermeer, The Netherlands

Year: 2002

Sqm: 1 250

The HydraPier sitting on the lake marks this tenuous threshold between land and water. Water is pumped over its roof and onto the vertical surfaces of its two 'water walls' in celebration of the area rich in history.

HydraPier is a covered landscape on the shore of the Haarlemmermeer Bos, an entrance bridge between the two water walls. It is also an enclosed multimedia exhibition space surrounded by a large deck that projects onto the lake. The architecture of the pavilion itself consists of two inclined, liquid covered metallic planes formed to incorporate an interior volume and an exterior pool. The planes become an architectural landscape that is a combination of natural and technological forces.

One enters this landscape below a glass pool that holds water at the five-meter level, marking the original water level. Continual pumping circulates water over the aluminum surfaces, and the controlled flow of water fuses with the wing like structure to create reflective, glistening and seemingly fluid surfaces. Air travelers above or visitors at ground level will see the pavilion's uplifted, liquid, wing-like roof reflect the sky by day, while at night they will see light and projected images emanating from it. Water is visible through the glazed underside of the pool as well as through the openings in the underside of the roof. The resultant spatial condition plays on the displacement of water relative to sea level and alludes to the artificial condition of the HydraPier's natural setting.

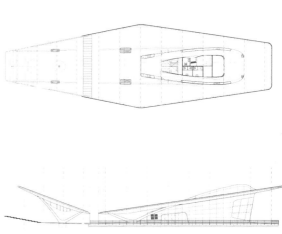

MIRRORS AND REFLECTION

THE BLIZARD BUILDING

Architect: Alsop Design Ltd/AMEC
Location: London, UK
Year: 2005
Sqm: 9 000

The building design has been developed around a core concept: to create a building which speaks about its purpose by providing a selectively transparent building envelope. Although direct views to the science areas are very carefully controlled, many of the functions of the building are visible to the passers-by.

The design team has worked with artists to create links between science and art within the fabric of the building. The gigantic glass panels which frame the bare steel structure designs by the award winning Bruce MacLean depict images of scientific themes. One goal was to create better science by breaking down the natural compartmentalisation of the separate departments by providing an open-plan environment, both in the laboratory and write-up areas.

The form and mass of the building are generated by a large, underground laboratory receiving large amounts of natural light from the glass pavilion above and roof-lights in the central mews area. The resulting plant wall is also a backdrop of light and art.

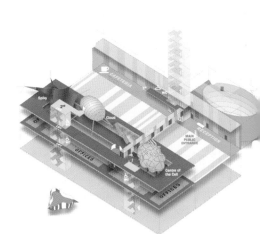

The building is distinguished by its adventurous use of colour. This includes the deep green pervasive throughout the lecture theatre, the pinks and the purples in the bridge link glazing, bold orange walls in the main entrance, deep red carpet throughout the glass pavilion, bright orange for centre of the cell pod and colourful artwork by Bruce McLean incorporated into the cladding.

LIGHT AND SHADOWS

"What is made by light casts a shadow and that shadow belongs to light", Architecture: Silence and Light, Louis Kahn

In the words of Kaoru Mende, renowned Japanese light designer, "To design shadows is to design light. No space exists without shadows." They make possible the perception of volume and shape in architecture. Mende's ideas for lighting projects for a given place stem from the shadows rather than from light. As with theatrical stage design, decisions need to be made as to which areas are to be brighter and which darker.

The Eastern world has always been more interested in this subject matter. The essay "In praise of shadows" (1933) by Junichiro Tanizaki explains how the sensibility towards shadows is one of the essential characteristics of traditional Japanese aesthetics. The Edo period, which led to the Meiji period at the end of the 19th century in Japan, is characterised, among other things, by its appreciation of darkness, seen as a quality brimming with potential that can induce serenity and delicacy. This culture also valued highly antique materials and old bronze pieces tinged green due to oxidation. Tanizaki explains how shadows are so important in interior design in his country: "The beauty of a Japanese room depends on a variation of shadows-heavy shadows against light shadows - it has nothing else. Westerners are amazed at the simplicity of Japanese rooms perceiving in them no more than ashen walls bereft of ornament. Their reaction is understandable, but it betrays a failure to comprehend the mystery of shadows."

The quality of the shadow - this region of darkness where the light is blocked - has a direct relation with its source. When the light is direct and intense the shadow will be dark and well defined. A more diffuse light will give more blurred shadows in gentle grey tones. This is known as half light and total darkness.

If there are diverse sources of light, the shadows will overlap, creating darker areas. When the lights are different colours, so are the shadows, except in the intersecting areas which are grey.

Their characteristics also depend on the relative situation between the light source, the object which is blocking the light, and the plane where the shadow is projected. The smaller the angle between the light direction and the surface onto which the shadow is cast, the longer the shadow will be. It will be bigger if there is a shorter distance between the object causing the shadow and the light source. All these effects are used in the Chinese shadow theatres.

Another interesting phenomenon related to shadow occurs when the light source is positioned behind the object which is being observed. This effect enhances the silhouette of objects, leaving the rest in darkness, and making details difficult to distinguish.

The Church of Light in Osaka (1987) designed by Tadao Ando is an impressive example of the possibilities of working with this technique in architecture. It is a concrete cube shaped space, in which light enters through a cruciform cut in the wall aligning perfectly with the joints in the concrete. The extension of the Novy Duur Monastery in the Czech Republic, by the architect John Pawson, a sensible minimalist volume with moving entries of light, is another remarkable example.

Architecture needs to take into account the fact that shadows change over the course of the day as evidence of the passing of time. Spaces change dramatically depending on how shadows are modified all day long. Perhaps, as Kaoru Mende declares, the work of the lighting designer consists in being able to structure the flow of time.

LIGHT AND SHADOWS

THREE ART MUSEUMS WIND, STONE AND WATER

Architect: Jun Itami
Location: Jeju Island, Korea
Year: 2005
Sqm: Wind 76; Stone 74; Water 192

The wind space is also associated with overlooked nature and memories. Designed using the concept of a hut, one elevation of this wooden box delineates the arc of a bow. As this arc incorporates a series of gaps between the wooden boards, wind passes through and sound is produced. With a solid stone object placed there as a stone chair, it is a meditation space where only the sound of the wind can be heard. By giving an entirely homogeneous coating to the interior, it emphasizes the light brought in through the slits.

The stone space has a single idea and poetic illusion. The stone artworks are shown inside a solid box, and in darkness. With intentionally opened holes like artificial flowers, and the movement of light coming in through these holes taking the lead role, this is a space of unlimited associations in the illusions they produce for the people viewing. By finishing the outer surface with wax, the color of steel is brought out as much as possible. Glass is fixed in the openings as if inserted with the steel plates, made so as not to obstruct the views from inside.

In the water space, materials native to this region were acquired, and an oval shape scooped from a strong cubic volume, with the movement of the sky reflected onto the surface of the water. Suggesting the beauty of overlooked nature, youth, and gravel glittering in the riverbed, it also expresses a smooth flowing sound.

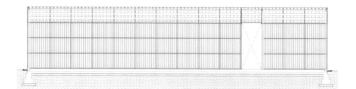

d Museum

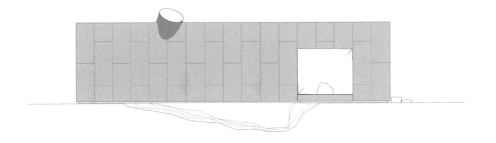

Stone Mus

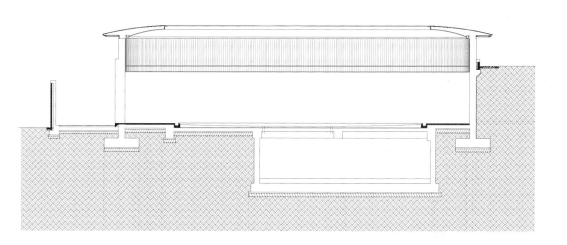

ater Museum

LIGHT AND SHADOWS

ART PAVILION

Architect: David Adjaye

Location: Island of San Lazzaro degli Armeni, Venice, Italy

Year: 2005

Sqm: 257

The main purpose of this Thyssen-Bornemisza 21st Century Art Pavilion is to create a dark internal space in a location where the natural light is exceptionally bright. In the artwork "Your black horizon" by Olafur Eliasson, a recording of the colour and intensity of the Venetian sky is projected at eye-level as a continuous band of light in which the cycle of one day is compressed into 15 minutes.

The pavilion was commissioned for this work and, to avoid breaking the projection, the floor of the main space is reached by a shallow ramp. Situated on an island in the Laguna, the spaces that lead the visitor from the water's edge to the dark interior make a sequential connection between the intensity of the arching sky and the equivalent intensity of Eliasson's projection. They also allow the eye to adjust to the different levels of illumination between the outside and the inside.

The construction employs prefabricated timber components clad in corrugated bituminous board, materials whose colour complements the blueness of the Laguna and the landscaping of the island.

In the light, our sense of place is based on a physical reading of the environment; in the dark, it is conditioned by a more acute awareness of our bodily position.

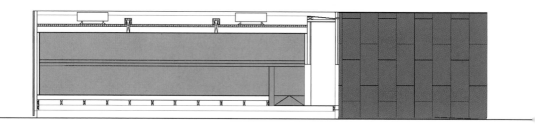

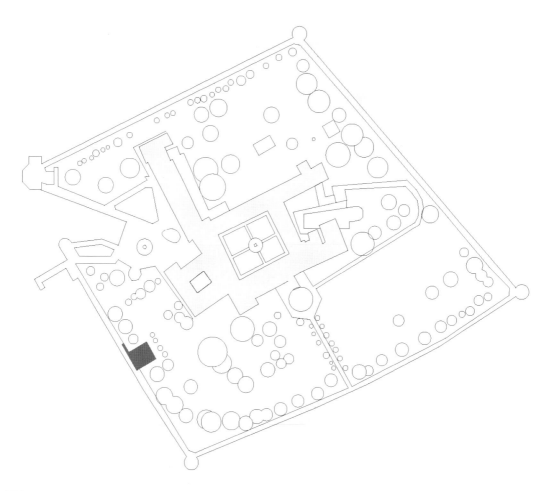

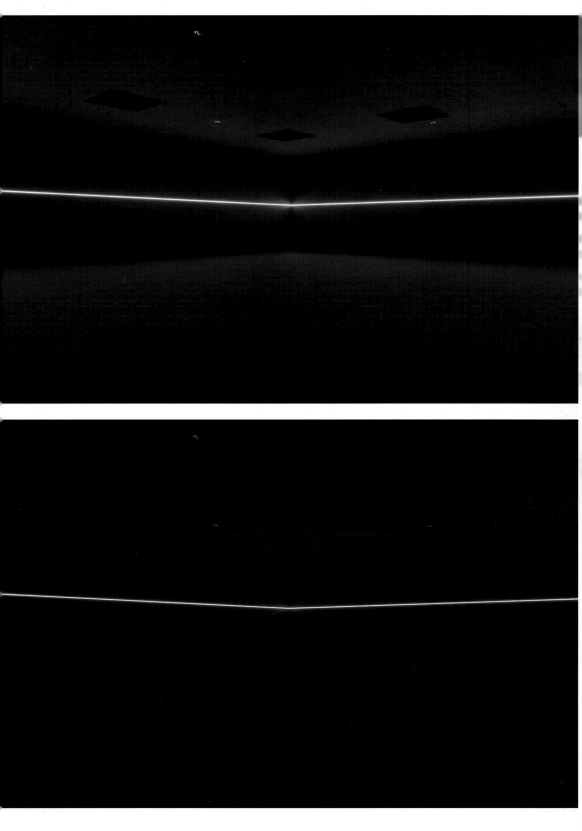

FACULTY OF ARTS LIBRARY MASARYK UNIVERSITY

Architect: Kuba & Pilar Architekti - Ladislav Kuba, Tomas Pilar
Location: Brno, Czech Republic
Year: 2005
Sqm: 589

The building of the library is situated in the middle of a heterogeneous city block, the housing of which developed during the 19th and 20th centuries. The library is designed to be a contrastive, simple building, thus expressing its specific mission and significance.

The facade of the building is comprised of a structural glazing system with an outer pane of toughened glass, a laminated inner pane of partially toughened clear glass and an opaque interlayer. This glazing, hung from pre-cast cantilevered ceiling slabs, forms part of a double facade system and hangs outside an inner masonry structure.

Openings within the masonry structure are formed by double glazed window units. Aluminium sheets are folded and welded to form the reveals with service hatches provided to access the ventilated service cavity with lighting behind.

The opaque part of the facade is lit from a ventilated cavity. The laminating interlayer of the glass provides distribution of the light from linear sources placed at the floor slabs of the cavity. The colour of the light is composed of the colour of the light sources, added coloured top foil of the cover and the colour of the glass' interlayer.

The abstract integrated area of the structured outer casing is accentuated by the conspicuous body of the entran
the entrance tube and the vertical tower of the lift shaft are underlined by a black-tinted glass facing. The wh
monolithic structure of the fire staircase at the south facade is encased in perpendicular steel rods.

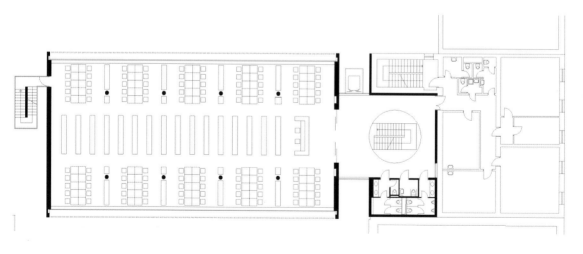

THE EFFECT
OF COLOUR

Underestimating the importance of colour is a common error in architecture. It has great influence on the final look of spaces and also on the way the people perceive them.

Colours can affect feelings, concentration and even health. Studies undertaken in offices and factories have demonstrated that the use of certain colours calms workers, reducing stress levels and improving overall efficiency. Today chromotherapy is used to study the benefits of colour on an organism. Although the effect of colour on a specific organ is difficult to quantify, there does exist a general psychology of colour. Goethe was already writing about the characteristics of colours and their effects on humans in his time. In her piece "The psychology of colour", Eva Heller states that the sensations or reactions created by colour are a universal rather than personal experience, and are linked to cultural, anthropological and even biological factors - given that colours develop sign value and this information is passed on through generations over time. Colours induce automatic and unconscious reactions and associations, for example, references to nature, such as forest/green or sea/blue. Every culture gives colours specific symbolic meanings and most of the times these meanings coincide. Warm colours like red, orange and yellow are seen as stimulating and jovial whereas cold blues and greens are deemed relaxing and serene. Red symbolizes fire and passion and sometimes violence as it is a stimulating colour. Yellow is normally linked to the sun and to feelings like happiness and vitality. Orange is a combination of these two colours and tends to share their qualities albeit to a lesser extent. Green is often linked to nature, knowledge and freshness whereas blue symbolizes serenity and the greatness of the sea and sky. Violet has a spiritual and delicate character and is simultaneously feminine and powerful.

Although black, white and grey are not considered to be colours by everybody, they also own a specific symbolism. In Western cultures, white represents innocence and black is usually a sign of mourning, sadness or death. Even though grey is made up of both black and white, its symbolism is somewhat distinct – it is associated with formality, resignation and boredom. Pink, brown, gold and silver (the latter two normally associated with opulence and wealth) are in a league of their own among the "psychological colours". The final effect of colour in décor will depend on the harmony and combination of secondary colours that surround the colour that is selected as a base. Chords of colour, or chromatic chords, similar to chords in music, will determine the kind of feelings that are provoked. For example, pink alongside cyan and white brings up feelings of innocence, and does not produce the same effect as it does next to red and black, where it symbolises provocation and sensuality.

In the design of a space, the tonality and saturation levels of the chosen colour should also be considered. For example, both cyan and ultramarine are blue, however their use will result in very different psychological and aesthetical consequences. Furthermore, the quality of light (its warmness), the orientation of the room, as well as the overall effect of the different tonalities that are chosen, have a great importance on the final ambience. Warm bright colours are recommended for north facing rooms as they bring comfort and a jovial spirit to the space. In areas which receive abundant direct light it is advisable to select a dark colour for one of the surface areas, such as the floor, to absorb some of the excess light and reduce visual fatigue. Colour can be used to help balance the characteristics of the lighting used in any given space.

Today, playing with the endless chromatic possibilities that exist and being creative with colour is a clear trend. This renewed interest in this matter has certainly been fuelled by the growing range of colours developed by the industry in many different materials.

THE EFFECT OF COLOUR

PALAIS DES CONGRES

Architect: Saia Barbarese Topouzanov Architectes
Location: Montreal, Canada
Year: 2003
Sqm: 110 000

Hovering above the urban gash create by the Ville Marie Expressway, the expansion of Montreal's Convention Centre aims to correct a break in the urban fabric that engages Old Montreal with the modern city. This addition restores the damaged urban tissue by filling in the former grade level and by creating much needed spaces of connection.

In the Palais des Congrès, the natural light is widely used to create a unique character for the building. The colourful elevation facing the Jean-Paul Riopelle Square animates the outdoor urban space and the interior simultaneously. During the day, the natural light that penetrates into the hall makes a fantastic world rich of a thousand colours, giving the impression that the visitor is bound inside an enormous kaleidoscope. The difference in the intensity of daylight throughout the seasons and at different times of the day creates variances in the atmosphere of the hall. At night, the elevation animates the square and glows as a jewel in the blue velvet of the sky. The circulation paths benefit from natural lighting a great deal and different means such as colours or other elements are used to either filter or transform daylight in order to diversify the experience.

A luminous marquee runs the length of the facade that forms the defining edge. This protects the decentralized entrance and, at the same time, creates an intermediate zone between the building and the exterior that encourages neighborly relations.

The transparency is articulated through the immense facade whose coloured glass panels create an interplay
light and colour, producing an iridescent effect both inside and outside the building.

ng the day, it is the array of colours that predominates, while the dark of night brings out its transparency.

To create a Palais open to the world, its city, and its people, the architectural concept focuses on the aspects of light and transparency with the use of three times more glassed surface area.

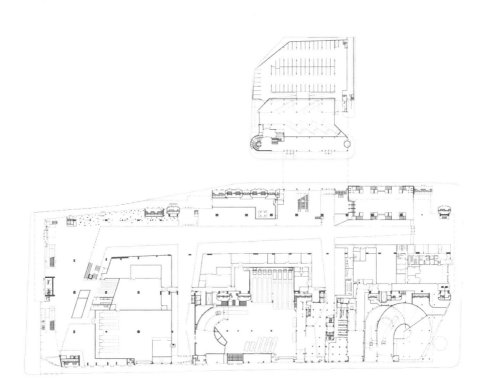

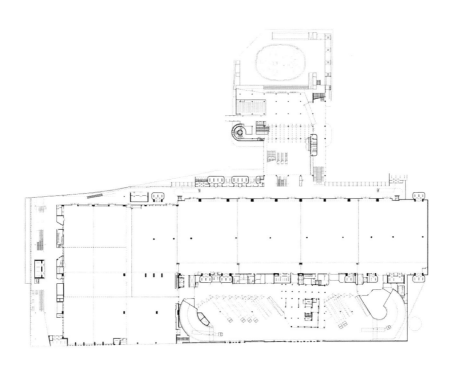

THE EFFECT OF COLOUR

WHITECHAPEL IDEA STORE

Architect: Adjaye/Associates
Location: London, UK
Year: 2005
Sqm: 3 440

The Whitechapel Idea Store is the flagship building for a programme based on a new type of information and learning provision which is being pioneered by the Borough of Tower Hamlets in London's East End. The external walls consist of storey-high panels which are fully glazed or incorporate thermal insulation. Available in several widths, they have been assembled with different proportions of solid to glazed panels to provide the thermal performance required of each facade. Stiffness is provided by laminated timber fins on the inside face of the wall and they also support bookshelves and worktops, depending on whether the wall is solid or glazed. The range of colours used for the glass is based on the colours of the striped fabric used to protect the nearby market stalls.

Internally, the proportions of the exposed concrete frame define a series of spaces which have a welcoming and inclusive character. On a smaller scale, the design of the light fittings, bookshelves and worktops creates a more intimate and changeful environment which is capable of addressing a wide range of expectations. By finding their inspiration in the local environment, Adjaye/Associates have succeeded in designing a a public building whose organisation and appearance are based on local, rather than imported, sources.

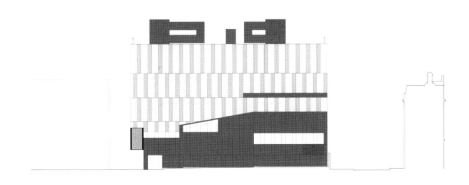

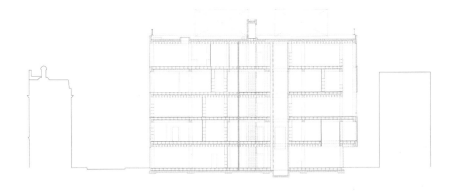

ARTIFICIAL LIGHTING

ARTIFICIAL LIGHTING

Artificial light is that which is produced by human technique. It transforms the daily cycle ruled by sunlight, conquering hours and dark places. Night time has never been the same since its arrival.

Cave fires were, most likely, the first kind of artificial light. Many years later light sources were developed using combustion in order to keep the light going longer, such as candles, oil, and petrol, kerosene and gas lamps.

At the close of the 19th century, Thomas A. Edison, after various experiments, invented the first incandescent light bulb. The way this light source works is simple: an electric current is transmitted through a filament within a protected area (glass bulb) which is either a vacuum or filled with an inert gas. In the first experiments, the filaments were made of carbon or of tantalum, shortly to be substituted by tungsten spiral filaments. As the current flows through the filaments, these become incandescent and at a temperature of 3000 °K they emit an optimum flow of light.

Incandescent light is the one most frequently used in the domestic environment given its warm and cosy qualities. Its installation is inexpensive without needing transformers or auxiliary equipment; it is small in size and can also be used in a wide variety of luminaries. On the downside, however, it is not very efficient in terms of units of light emitted and energy consumed (lm/W). The incandescence also produces, as well as light, a large amount of thermal energy, which means it uses up more electricity resulting in higher running costs. Another disadvantage is its short useful life: over time the tungsten in the filament evaporates and shrinks in size until it is too fragile to transmit the current and it finally breaks. Its average life span is approximately 1000 hours.

PAR (parabolic aluminized reflector) incandescent lights substantially increase the efficiency of the more classic incandescent light sources and also boost the standard duration to approximately 1500 hours.

The development of halogen light signifies yet another step forward in the search for a good chromatic reproduction. In this case, the introduction of a trace of halogen, often in the form of iodine, into the enclosed gassy environment of the tungsten filament gives the bulb a longer life and enhances its chromatic reproduction quality. A further convenience is the use of dimmer switches which easily control the intensity of the light. Among the halogen light sources there are those which work in standard light fittings of incandescent light and those of low voltage. The latter are quite efficient with reasonable running costs. However, they do need an electric voltage transformer (which is not always easy to conceal) and they give off a great deal of thermic energy. These types of light sources are commonly used in retail interior design. It is without a doubt the preferred lighting in shop window displays.

Fluorescent lamps are the most common in offices and also in commercial spaces, car parks, and so on. In these kind of lamps the electric discharge is not produced in a filament, but through a glass tube filled with gas (usually krypton or argon), with an interior coating of phosphor dust. The electric discharge induces the gas to emit radiations which interact with the phosphor to make it shine and project light. The light quality produced by the fluorescent light greatly depends on the exact composition of the coating. It has the reputation of being a cold, bluish, and unattractive light with little contrast. However, advances are being made and today fluorescents can have very acceptable chromatic reproductions. They are efficient durable light sources with minimum thermic energy losses and overall very economical. Among the disadvantages are its slow start up, the gradual loss of quality and an annoying flickering effect in some cases. Its most normal shape is the long tube; however the development of compact fluorescent lamps enables them to be fitted in smaller spaces and so widens the possibilities of its usage.

The most efficient lamps are the mercury discharge lamps and the high and low pressure sodium lamps which are generally used in urban and industrial lighting.

The low pressure sodium lamps emit a monochromatic light of yellow tones which does not reproduce the colour of the objects it illuminates. This kind of light is most widely used in road and motorway lighting. Other types of lamps include the mixed light lamp, the induction lamps (highly efficient) and cathode light tubes. Cathode light is available in many colours and is popular in luminous advertising.

Artificial light is a field in permanent development and awash with innovations, such as LED lights or fibre optic lighting. The ever growing variety of available options gives way to an unlimited amount of possible lighting effects. The ability to control the characteristics of light, such as its intensity, direction, quality and colour, is also increasing.

In artificial lighting, besides choosing the most appropriate type of light source, it is essential to select the right kind of illumination, as well as the light fittings that are best suited to achieve the desired effects. There are numerous possible classifications when dealing with artificial light. One relates to the direction of the light projection, where the lighting is divided in direct, mixed or indirect. Another refers to its main function: ambiance lighting, task-lighting, or emergency lights. Illumination can also be classified according to the way it is distributed throughout the space, where it can be general, supplementary or focussed on one area. In practice, these concepts are not separate, and it is advisable to experiment with imagination and sensitivity rather than to limit oneself rigidly to these categories. It is no doubt an area with enormous expressive possibilities and a creative potential that is becoming more and more relevant in contemporary architecture.

LINEAR LIGHT

It is not simple to speak rigorously about the effects of something as elusive and full of unsuspected nuances as light. The different possible classifications for studying it usually fall short when describing the illumination of a space, where diverse phenomena can occur simultaneously. It then becomes difficult to separate and measure. Therefore, this chapter on "linear" light is really dealing with a type of illumination in which "linearity" is paramount, without forgetting that light's own characteristics result in secondary light effects.

In artificial illumination a distinction must be established between light-emitting bodies, light radiation emitted, and surfaces which reflect and absorb these radiations. Many interior designers and technicians try to conceal the light source when using fluorescent lighting, neon lighting or linestra lamps, especially in domestic settings or certain types of commercial spaces. Walls or other surfaces are normally used to "bathe" the space in light, creating indirect illumination.

On other occasions, fluorescent tubing or neon lights are visible and form an important part of the composition. In the 20th century, artists such as Dan Flavin, rather than architects or interior designers, have been at the forefront of the study of the eye-catching effects to be attained by the careful use of these light sources. Their colour, intensity and longitude, as well as the geometric and material properties of the surfaces onto which light is projected, are the qualities to be considered. Since the early sixties, Dan Flavin (1933-1996) investigated the expressive possibilities of fluorescent lights - works of art which were made with economical tubes, easy to find on the market and to replace. This is why his work is often included, perhaps incorrectly, in the minimalist trend (such as the homage to Tatlin). Oddly, today the tubes with which he created his first works are no longer made, meaning that his pieces are not replaceable and have been converted into the type of sacred and untouchable personal art which the minimalists criticized in the sixties. For Flavin, his works did not just stop at the layout of fluorescent lights in a minimalist manner, but went beyond that - they are an interaction between the light and the space where it is projected, which searches for a spiritual vibration. The analysis of this type of illumination has uncovered many of its possibilities. The work, "Untitled", made by Flavin in 1966, consists of "a fluorescent square" placed in a corner which alters the perception of the whole room, dematerialising its edges.

The combination of different shades can be unexpected, and a balanced mix produces white light. The fluorescent green and white are the brightest, given the mix of phosphors in the glass tube filled with mercury vapour, which makes up the fluorescent lamp. On the other hand, the red fluorescent lights are duller as the tube is dyed which obstructs some of the light flow.

In architecture, "linear" illumination can be used to enhance the longitudinal qualities of a space, such as in the Sines Cultural Centre projected by the architects Aires Mateus, where distances seem to grow perceptively because of the illumination. This kind of lighting also aids in determining the directionality of a place, indicating the way for those who go through the space. It is a type of illumination which inspires fluid and dynamic atmospheres, such as those of the Zaha Hadid buildings, for example the Strasbourg Interchange. The ceiling of the PJ NHK Nagano Station which is lit up by endless rows of fluorescent lights helps the users move in an orderly manner, in the same way as the flashing white lines of motorways.

Other architects use fluorescent lighting to a more sculptural end, such as Daniel Libeskind, who searches for the ambiguous, creating false incisions which divide the spaces, blending them with the real openings which connect to the exterior.

LINEAR LIGHT

CENTRO DE ARTES DE SINES

Architect: Manuel Aires Mateus, Francisco Aires Mateus
Location: Sines, Portugal
Year: 2005
Sqm: 8 065

The building is situated at the start of the main street linking the town to the sea and marking the traditional entrance to the historic nucleus. The Centre subsumes diverse activities capable of generating an exceptional building: exhibition rooms, a library, a cinema-cum-theatre and a documentation centre. The wide-ranging program calls for the whole plot to be occupied, enveloping the street below the main ground level and adapting its exterior volume to the monumental scale of the castle walls. The four modules are set out on the upper floors in parallel bands intercalated with patios. The decks were hung from a bridge-like structure supported on the perimetral walls alone. This system allows a spatial configuration on the basement level that is adapted to the dimensions of the common areas; at street level it guarantees an unbroken view right through the inside of the building, including the activity of the Centre in the daily life of the town.

The ingenious use of fluorescent lights mark a strong directionality in the interior space.

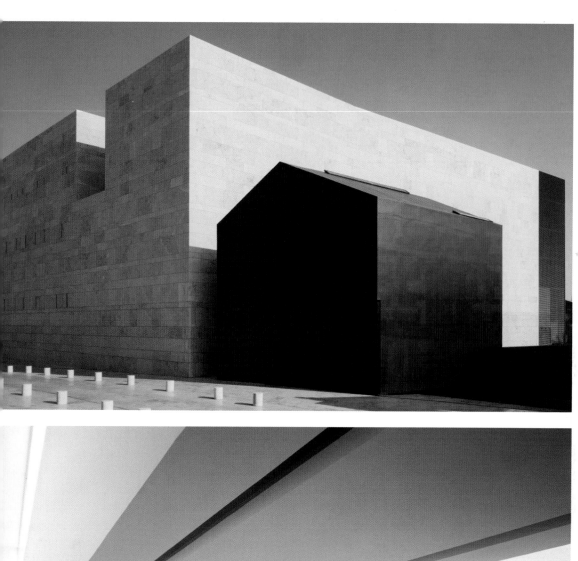

It appears as if the Arts Centre has been fused, quite deliberately and with great precision, into the tightly built-up urban environment of the Portuguese port of Sines.

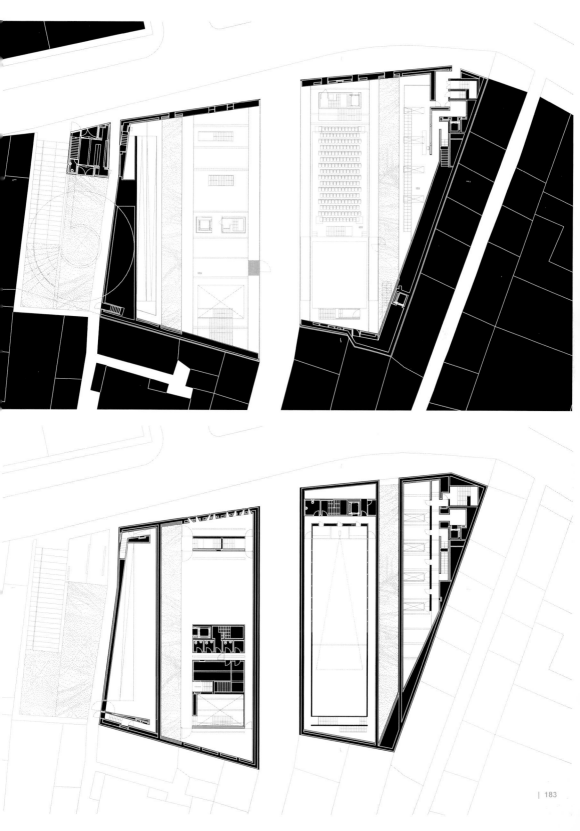

LIGHT SURFACES

Artificial lighting and its expressive and artistic possibilities are evermore apparent in the contemporary architectural scene. The study of illumination of a building was for years limited to solving the functional and safety problems. The main objective of these projects, normally carried out by engineers who were experts in illumination, was to guarantee a standard light flow depending on the usage (for example, the DIN standard requires 500 luxes for office spaces). The homogeneity of light was considered to be a positive characteristic. These basic needs of course still need to be met; however, illumination projects have become much more conceptual, aesthetically more sophisticated and demanding when aiming to create a certain atmosphere.

Planes of light, plastic panels or glass lit up by fluorescent lighting and other types of lamps are all commonly used elements in today's architecture. These kinds of lighting draw inspiration from the luminous advertising boards which continue their advertising role at night time. In order to unify the superficial light, the diffusing surface (usually of translucent materials) is normally situated at a certain distance from the fluorescent tubing (the minimum would be between 10 and 15 cm). Between each fluorescent tube there should be a distance of between 15 and 25 cm. These light fixtures which are relatively economical and easy to assemble are visually effective and aesthetically pleasing.

A clear example is the shop and art gallery created by the Carmenzind Grafensteiner architects in Zurich. It is a minimalist and anonymous prism of two floors which does not instantly attract attention during daylight hours. However, at night, the building is transformed and the upper floor is converted into luminous parallel pipes which look as though they are suspended in the air. Buildings are converted into urban lamps, with all the advantages and disadvantages this represents. On the positive side, these planes of light on the facade bring vitality to the streets they illuminate. The downside is, of course, the light pollution and the potential energy costs if badly managed. Today, however, a gentle illumination using LEDs would be able to adequately solve these two problems.

Another interesting example is the restoration of the Bankside Power Station in London which was converted into the Tate Modern by the architects Herzog and de Meuron. The project, presented at an international competition in 1994, was the winning choice given the intelligent way in which they made the most of the existing conditions. The project can be described as the emptying of the existing space and its illumination by the means of boxes of light. These prisms of light, which are lit by fluorescent lamps, bring a truly contemporary feel to the old turbine hall, which is converted into a new atrium for culture.

The Ostfilden Town Hall in Germany, designed by Jurgen H Mayer, which received a special mention at the 2003 Mies van der Rohe Prize, is yet another example of a building with a spectacular display of planes of light. An impressive porch which projects white light welcomes the visitor into the building. In the interior, ceilings, corridors and stairwells are all luminous in form and emit a clear and uniform light, creating a futuristic atmosphere, reminiscent of Stanley Kubrick's film *2001: A Space Odyssey*. The use of these types of surfaces has been one of the principal trends in architecture and interior design in the beginning of this 21st century.

LIGHT SURFACES

ALFRED LERNER HALL STUDENT CENTRE

Architect: Bernard Tschumi Architects in association
with Gruzen Samton Associated Architects
Location: Columbia University, New York City, USA
Year: 1999
Sqm: 22 500

The exterior envelope of the student centre, in its massing and its "image," respects and reinforces the intentions of the historical context. The two principal wings, which face Broadway and the campus, remain faithful to the master plan by McKim, Mead, and White and the materials of the existing campus, which are primarily brick and granite. The student centre translates the exterior public courtyard which the McKim plan had intended to place between the wings into a linked series of enclosed spaces for the public elements of program. These spaces include the main, multifunctional student lounge (or "Hub"), the auditorium and the theatre. To tie all of these programs into the activity of the central campus (which remains the true "centre" of student activities), they are separated from campus by only a glass wall that stretches between the two wings, using state-of-the-art technology to maximize the transparency of its materials.

While the building's exterior returns to its original context for inspiration, the building's innovative interior accommodates the needs of student life at a large contemporary university. Located directly behind the glass curtain wall, the Hub is the student centre's main space of social and circulatory exchange. It is comprised of a dual system of opposed ramps that link the split-level wings into a continuous circuit, thereby joining traditionally dissociated, disparate floors and activities into a space of fluid communication. It is simultaneously a void (the void of McKim's plan) and a route. During the day, light filters through the suspended glass ramps. At night, as light glows from the inside, figures in movement along this route will appear as if in a silent shadow theatre.

This space of exchange — one of the key, non-localizable functions of a student centre — is also an exhibition space; it is the spillover from bar, game room, mailroom and theatre.

LIGHT SURFACES

BROADWAY CINEPLEX

Architect: Edge Design
Location: Hong Kong, China
Year: 1997
Sqm: 1 200

The design brief for this new eight-screen multiplex cinema, located in the new town of Tin Shui Wai, highlighted the need to create a sense of coherent unity. The eight theatres were divided into groups of two "twins" and located in two different buildings separated by a major thoroughfare that runs across a shopping complex. The conceptual idea, provided by an existing mirror plan, developed from the metaphor of "twins" and the idea that even "identical" twins are not exactly the same but rather variations or reflections of each other.

Light and colour became the main architectural elements used in creating individual but related identities. The two groups of theatres were conceived as glowing objects floating within the shell of the reflective, curtain-wall glass buildings. By day the glass is visually impenetrable, mirroring the opposite building and surrounding towers. As the sun goes down the facade gradually becomes more transparent, revealing the strongly lit elements inside, challenging and blurring the boundary between inside and outside. A glowing bar, situated at the end of a double-height lobby hall, draws the waiting visitors to the curved window facade. The use of a localised lighting system, with emphasis on various colours of fluorescent lights and textures rather than materials and finishes, made it possible to stay within a very low budget for the relatively vast spaces.

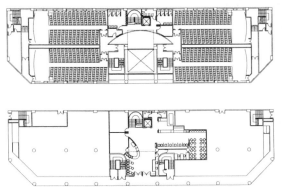

LIGHT SURFACES

TYRE SHOP - ART EXCHANGE

Architect: Camenzind Gräfensteiner Architects
Location: Zurich, Switzerland
Year: 2000

The new tyre fitting shop / art exchange is situated on a brownfield site adjacent to the lake of Zurich. The client was looking for a highly efficient tyre-fitting workshop with a strong visual identity.

Movement is the key, which drives this ever-changing environment. Therefore, the entire facade of the first floor of this tyre-fitting building was conceived as a four-sided, 200 sqm interactive communication surface. Sponsored by tyre manufacturers, young artists are given the opportunity to challenge the borders of art by taking their work out of the gallery and placing it into a commercial, fast moving environment. Challenging the conventional frontiers of art and commerce, the building becomes a marker of the cultural identity of today.

Practical and elegant, this little tyre-changing shop is a banal building type that has been transformed into an illuminated signal for entrance to the centre.

The building was constructed
a steel frame with concrete flo
and insulated metal tray pan
covered with a layer of glass
rain screen cladding. The bu
ing has been awarded with
Building of Excellence Award.

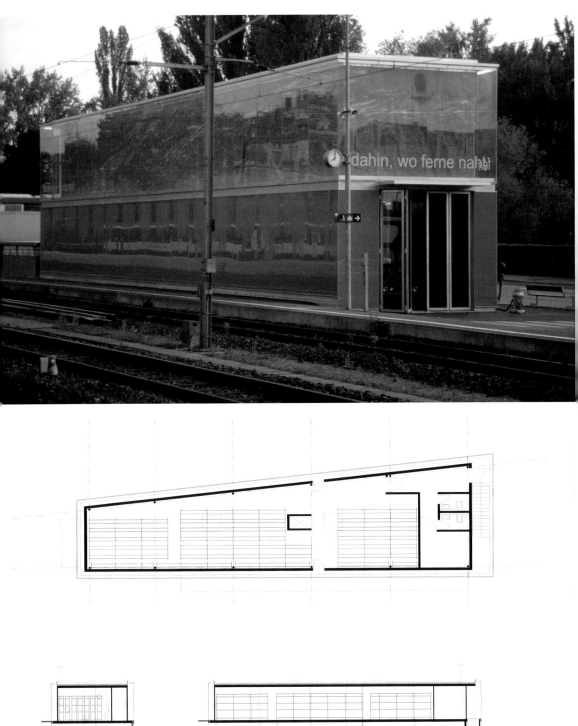

On the first floor, the metal panels were set back from the glass facade to create a 50 cm wide access space in which to install artwork.

LIGHT SURFACES

TOWNHALL OF OSTFILDERN STADT.HAUS

Architect: J. Mayer H. Architects
Location: Ostfildern, Germany
Year: 2001
Sqm: 1 100

Stadt.haus is located at the centre of Scharnhauser Park, a former American military site next to Stuttgart Airport. It is a multifunctional public building. Spatially the entire building is considered as a large, open public space with inlays of certain core elements. Floating within a space for mutual or strategic communication, these enclosed boxes structure the interior layout of the building. From the main square to the panorama deck on the roof, the stadt.haus interlocks with its context through cutouts and terraces. These open air spaces remain accessible beyond the main opening hours and therefore serve as spatial and programmatic extensions.

Light and water animations are integral parts of the stadt.haus and include a subtle relationship between nature and technology. The stadt.haus and square construct a new public building prototype by offering simultaneity of city life in real, mediated and virtual space.

Framing the main entrance visitors will have to walk through computer animated artificial rain dripping from underneath the flat cantilevered roof. This water curtain facade becomes a secret information producer treating the entry elevation as ephemeral skin.

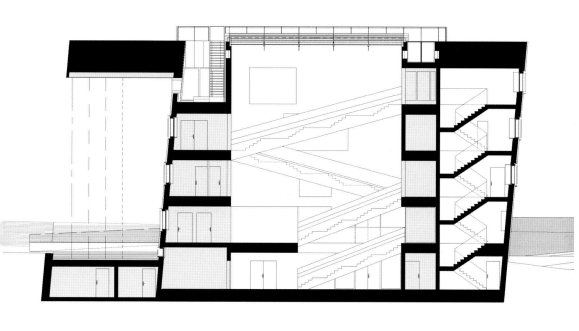

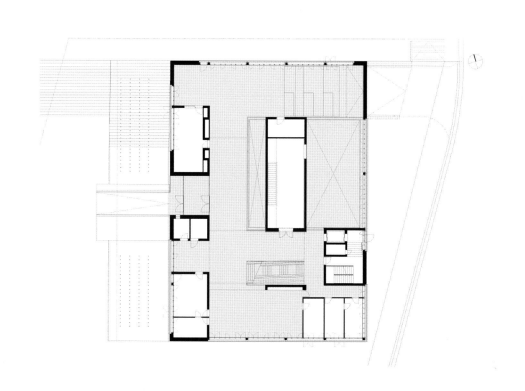

LIGHT SURFACES

EUROPARK 2 INSELN

Architect: Massimiliano Fuksas
Location: Salzburg, Austria
Year: 2003
Sqm: 15 000

The project is based on the dynamic analysis of flux and the study of its origins. Europark II is divided into two parts: the expansion of the existing shopping center and the landscape design of the area surrounding the Europark.

Made from grilled metal, the wave covering is the architectural relief motif for this vast, recently completed project that takes up an area of 120,000 square meters dedicated to commercial space and parking for 3000 automobiles.

The suggestive allusion to one element - the sea, that is not to be found in Austria - is the element of covering, strongly characterized. It gives shelter to the parking places and at the same time acts as a sign of great remembrance. The continuity of this element finds its counterpoint in the dynamic disposition and the tension of the lower volumes determined by the force of the interior "empty space" that are reserved for commercial activities. In the southern part of the area, enriched with vegetation, a refined play of reflections between the large walls and serigraphed glass of the commercial center and the pool of water crossed by paths, demonstrate again Fuksas' particular constructive sensibility with regard to "light" and "transparency."

The shopping centre is divided into two storeys - two glazed volumes that are penetrated by curved shapes and islands.

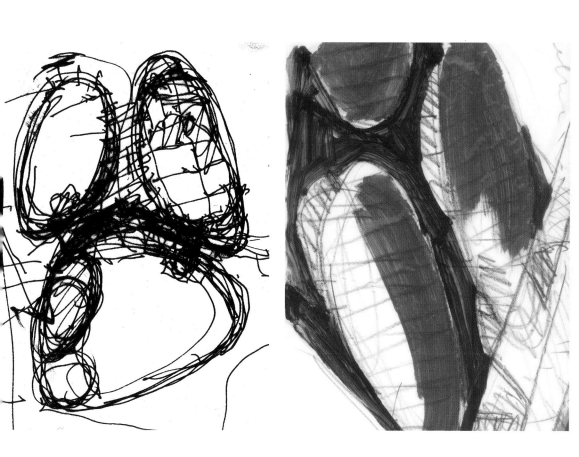

e car park at the roof level
covered by a variety of fluid
apes recalling the islands
ow, which become the focal
nts of the new complex.

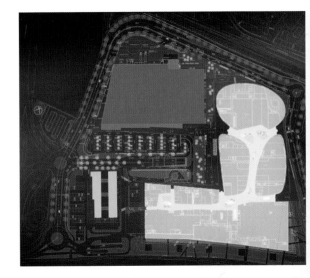

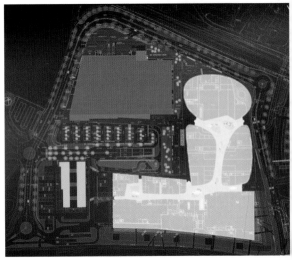

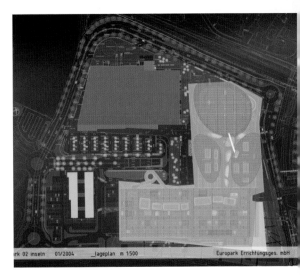

rk 02 inseln   01/2004   _lageplan m 1:500   Europark Errichtüngsges. mbH

LIGHT FILTERS

The flow of excessive direct light into a space can be uncomfortable. A large contrast between light and shadow may cause dazzling and even visual fatigue. Curtains and blinds have long been used to prevent such situations and, besides filtering the light, provide the interior space with greater intimacy.

Light is easily manipulated by using filters of different materials, enabling a large part of its characteristics to be altered- its direction, colour, shade and the kind of projection it produces in the space. The fact that both natural light and artificial light can be modified in this manner has resulted in the unlimited development of lamps and luminaries ever since the invention of the electric light bulb. Soon after, it became clear that by concealing the light bulb with something, such as a shade, visual comfort was increased.

As an object of design, the lamp is an industrial product which enjoys great popularity. Among its advantages is the capability of adding interest and personality to more or less dull spaces. However, the growing tendency among illumination specialists is to integrate the lighting into the architecture itself, at times concealing the light sources. The quality of light, rather than the design of luminaries, is the most important in the actual lighting projects. In this way, the study of the illumination becomes part of the architectural project, strengthening the aesthetics of the different planes and volumes and completing the general concept rather than being developed as an afterthought.

In this context, some walls are converted into large illuminated surfaces which bathe the space in light. This is sometimes achieved by a series of fluorescents covered by a material that acts as a filter, like translucent glass or methacrylate. The material used to filter the light sets the tone of the place. The possibilities are infinite – the only condition is that the chosen filter or combination allows some of the light to flow through.

The development of new materials and systems for modifying the features of closures has greatly widened the field of experimentation. Some have truly influenced the architecture of the past decade, such as the incorporation of stainless steel and copper metallic meshing with high quality finishes, the introduction of glass treated with an extensive variety of filters and colours and the use of durable textile materials.

On a larger scale, whole buildings are covered with perforated delicate materials which illuminate the urban landscape. As opposed to their traditional robust and immutable look, buildings are now being designed as though dressed in silk and chiffon – complete with subtle and variable transparencies, depending on the light flow.

The most important aspect of the facade/filter is that it separates the desired elements, like illumination and ventilation, from the undesired elements – glare, excessive heat, and the physical and visual interference – as well as being aesthetically pleasing.

FLON RAILWAY
AND BUS STATION

Architect: Bernard Tschumi Architects
Location: Lausanne, Switzerland
Year: 2001
Sqm: 3 500

Located in the heart of the Flon Valley at the Place de l'Europe, this station is the beginning of a new infrastructure network of transportation systems that will link Lausanne's center to its suburban peripheries. Four different lines of commuter services converge on the group of rectilinear steel-framed structures, sheathed in red-printed glass. The first phase, inaugurated and put into service in early spring 2001, consists of the regional train and bus stations, elevators, a glass-enclosed bridge and a new traffic circle. Phase two will include a subway station, escalators with a glass envelope and an oblique plaza.

Part of a master plan won in competition in 1988, the project developed from the distinctive hilly topography of Lausanne, where streets appear as if suspended, buildings seem either buried in the ground or like vertical passageways and bridges serve as multi-storey crossings. One of four "inhabited bridges" proposed in the master plan, the Interface transport system links different parts of the city, while its ramps, escalators and elevators connect the lower levels of the valley (currently filled with industrial warehouses) with the upper levels of the historical city.

The different parts of the station are conceived as movement vectors in a dynamic circulation system that carries Lausanne's citizens and neighbors through a complex of transportation, commerce and civic enlightenment. The parts of this system are multivalent: bridges are walkways and departure areas; the trainside platforms serve as streets; the public plaza provides an urban garden.

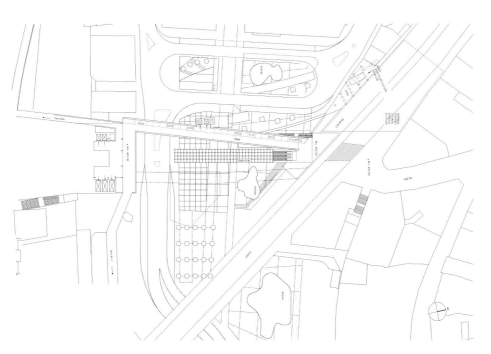

NATIONAL CHOREOGRAPHIC CENTRE

Architect: Rudy Ricciotti
Location: Aix-en-Provence, France
Year: 2006
Sqm: 2 675

In the beginning the need for open floors, completely free of constraints, required the shift of the structural load to the facades. In order to avoid walls or interior pillars, the choice of a great range of floors was evident.

Ricciotti consciously espouses the heavy, rough and low tech in a kind of architectural arte povera. However, for this latest building, a contemporary dance centre in Aix-en-Provence, there are signs that he is lightening up. The signature dark concrete structure is still evident, but here it is reworked as a cage of thick, angular sinews that form a protective armature to a more delicate glazed volume behind. Like a dancer's body, the concrete has a lean yet muscular quality and its lattice-like geometry filters light and casts dramatic shadows across the floors of the dance studios.

Squeezed into a tight, sloping site, the glazed box is tautly raked and caressed by angular ribs of charcoal concrete. But this is not simply another gratuitous device. On the lower levels, the blind box of the theatre anchors the composition, with one floor of offices and two floors of double-height dance studios stacked above. As the building rises, so it becomes physically and experientially lighter, reflected in the gradual tapering of the structural ribs. At either end the concrete cage is braced and bulwarked by partly exposed stair towers.

A centre of creation, the NCC vibrates between transparency and light.

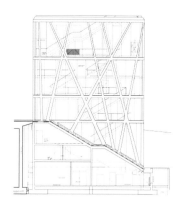

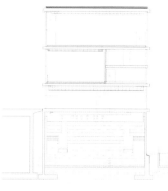

BT CELLNET 02 MOBILE APPLICATIONS DEVELOPMENT AND IMPLEMENTATION CENTRE

Architect: Eldridge Smerin Architects
Location: London, UK
Year: 2003
Sqm: 800

BT Cellnet/02 appointed Eldridge Smerin to design their new temporary research headquarters in Ealing, West London in 2001 following a design competition. Eldridge Smerin's proposal responded to the fact that BT Cellnet's studio was due for demolition in two years time and centred on the design of elements that could be taken away and re-used in a new building.

The design of the open plan work area challenges the conventions of BT's corporate environment providing a model for application development facilities of this kind within the firm's new organisation.

Eldridge Smerin wrapped the entire exterior in a white translucent fabric skin presenting a new and quite abstract image to the outside world and protecting the centre from the adjacent construction sites. Internally, apart from the creation of dramatic new volumes and incisions in the brick structure, a minimal amount of works were carried out to the existing building.

Eldridge Smerin worked closely with theatrical lighting and sound specialists to create a unique work environment with a programmable lighting and sound system.

This was a flexible, economical solution designed and constructed in a six month period.

PERFORATIONS

A perforation is an opening in a surface through which light can flow. Although any window in a wall represents an opening, it is only considered to be a perforation when the size of the aperture is sufficiently reduced in relation to the surface area of the wall. These perforations allow buildings to conserve their massive and robust aspect.

Perforations are usually big enough to allow light to flow into a closed space but generally not big enough to allow views from the outside. In oriental tradition they are used to illuminate domes. According to the architect Elias Torres, the points of light in spaces covered by domes are a sign of the poetic nostalgia of an interior space protected from the immenseness of the firmament. Perforations in roofs often symbolize stars and many Arab baths are illuminated in this way. The steam can enhance the rays of light in a dramatic manner which adds to the mystery of where the light originates. To recreate the light of stars, the spectator can be fooled by electrical light and perforated false ceilings; then, zenithal light is not necessary.

During the Sixties, the Argentinean artist Lucio Fontana studied the potential of perforations. In Italy, from 1960 onwards, he developed the series, "Spatial concepts," which involves a series of monochrome sheets of fabric punctured or ripped by the artist. This work immortalized him in the history of art and represented, for him, the introduction of a third dimension by using holes and cuts. The result is a surprising nexus which merges the front and back part of the material.On a far larger scale, the artist Gordon Matta-Clark also experimented with the unpredictable spatial and visual connections which can be created by large holes that perforated at the same time walls, ceilings and floors, made in tumble-down buildings. In architecture, perforations differ from windows in their apparent unpremeditated nature.

The window is a main element of architectural composition – the geometric balance between full and empty – and in a way, a product and representation of human reason. On the other hand, the orifice is more related to nature, reminiscent of places created by geology, such as caverns and caves, decomposition processes, or biological actions such as the work of ants, termites and other insects.

In its search for new aesthetics, contemporary architecture is returning, paradoxically, to organic and archaic inspired elements. Although technology can provide enormous lights and glass curtain walls, the sight of a large, informally perforated wall, like the Mikimoto building in Ginza (Japan), by architect Toyo Ito, may be more suggestive.

With this resort, the building is able to maintain its closed protective nature. It is an ideal feature for intimate spaces built for contemplation like churches and museums. They help to highlight the thickness, weight and volume of the wall - creating a strong contrast with the immateriality and spirituality of the light which flows through them.

At night time, the direction of the light is inverted and the apertures become points of light. An interesting example can be seen in the Louis Vuitton shop in Ginza, Japan built in 2004 by the architect Jun Aoki.

PERFORATIONS

LOUIS VUITTON GINZA NAMIKI

Architect: Jun Aoki & Associates (exterior)
Interior design: Louis Vuitton Malletier
Location: Chuo-ku, Tokyo
Year: 2004
Sqm: 266

The project entailed the complete renovation, interior and exterior, of a building located in the commercial district of Ginza. The new facade is composed of imitation limestone panels of GRC (Glass Fiber Reinforced Concrete), with inlaid translucent white marble. A steel frame fixes the panels onto the structure. Marble squares (2cm, 6cm, 15cm, 1m) have been randomly laid down. The GRC panels' thickness varies: 35mm in the opaque area and 20mm in the semi-transparent and bright area, alike marble. The arrangement of all marble plates was present on the elevation drawings. The layout had to be precise in order to avoid the shade caused by equipment stored behind the panels.

Sheets of glass fiber fitting the marble plates were laid at the rear as to give the facade the appearance of natural texture. Then cement was cast and polished. Consequently, huge manual procedures were taken up to achieve such amazing stone like panels. By day, the building appears as a simple 20m long, 16m wide, 21m high volume. However, by night, its multiple squares materialize on the surface. The exterior wall, distinct from either the interior or the structure, was taken up as an independent design territory.

The nocturnal image of this large volume illuminated by small squares of light is truly impressive.

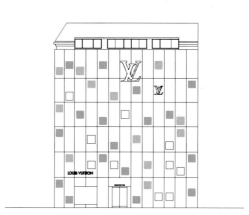

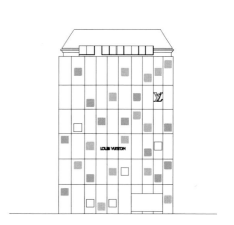

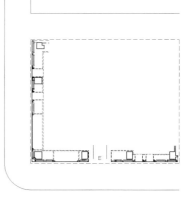

PERFORATIONS

CONSEJO REGULADOR RIBERA D. DUERO

Architect: Estudio Barozzi Veiga, Fabrizio Barozzi, Alberto Veiga
Location: Roa, Spain
Year: 2008
Sqm: 3 624

The interpretation, as the principal search, gives the capacity for the desire for knowledge that sustains the whole of artistic expression, while architecture, as a practicing art, can only be expressed constitutionally as interpretation, and the real is its space of knowledge. As such, the project is simply founded as a unique interpretation of the reality of its place. The place has been carved by the city and the landscape, and the project simply interprets this condition, outlining the difference that brings us closer to understanding.

From this element, the project becomes independent and moves towards the large scale and the distant landscape, defining an independent element and able to confront the distance. An emerging element provides continuity with the context and its iconic elements and establishes a dialogue with the horizon of the plateau and the monumentality of the landscape, identifying itself as a timeless monolith.

To filter the light, guide it and blur it, they tried to give it a volume that achieves an atmosphere and works with this atmosphere. To convert the light elements in another element of the work, a physical element, guides us to a specific treatment of the openings. The irregular blured openings in the elevations allow us to formally transform the interior spaces, spaces sifted by light filters - filters that could represent the inner contrast to the exterior space.

The materiality of the project, local stone, is seen as an intensification of the place's character, allowing a subquent sensory evocation of the landscape. The treatment of the openings suggests and opens up the space difference, positioning the project in a radically contemporary condition.

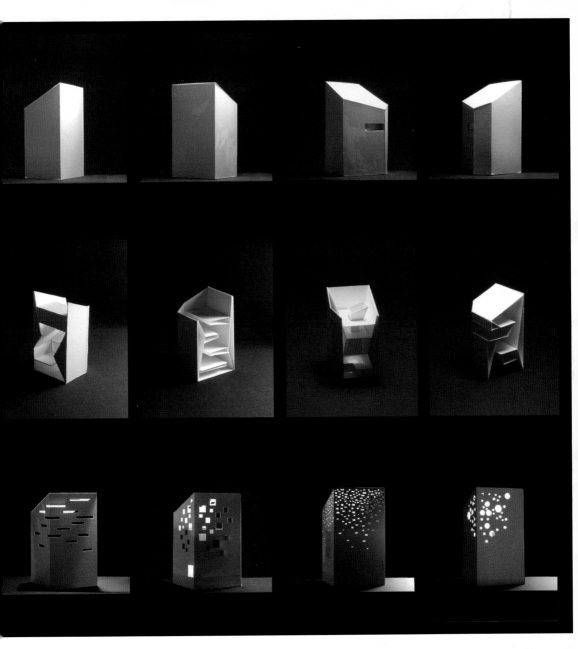

building moves in between those double tensions: it moves as it follows, and adapts and finds an architectonic
n for the meanings that synthesize the city and the landscape. The project becomes a material conclusion of
existing volume, suggesting the need for a conclusive element that expresses the temporary disconnection
he new volume. This new element forms a dependent one, follows the lines of the old element and declares the
possibility of an authentic redefinition of its historic appearance.

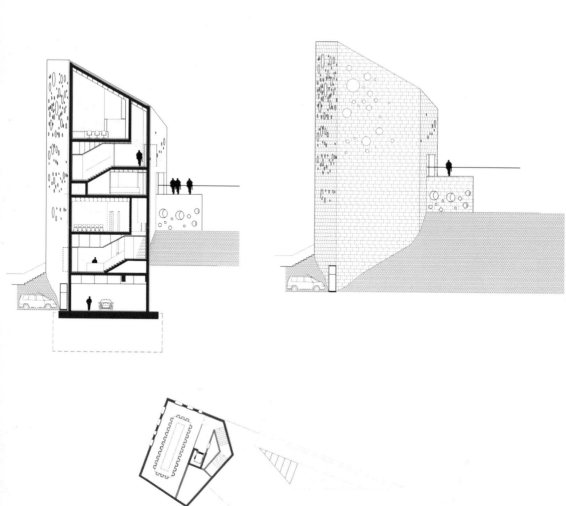

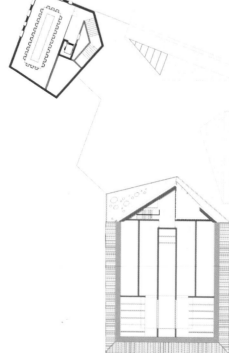

PERFORATIONS

ESPACIO DE CREACION ARTISTICA CONTEMPORANEA

Architect: Nieto Sobejano Arquitectos, S.L.

Conception & design of the lighting facade: realities:united.

Location: Cordoba, Spain

Year: under construction - 2008

Facade surface aprox.: 1 300

The winning competition entry for the "Espacio de Creación Artística Contemporánea" by Nieto Sobejano architects from Spain proposed the integration of a light and media facade on the building surface facing the Río Guadalquivir.

Realities:United was commissioned to develop the conception and the design for this media skin.

The facade made from pre-cast fiber concrete panels (GRC) has been transformed into a three-dimensional relief with indented "bowls" which are an abstract derivate of the interior structure of the building. The indirectly lit "bowls" are arranged in patterns of varying density and respectively element size. They result in a screen with a varying image resolution similar to the retina of the human eye. The grayscale system based on fluorescent light will allow the display of moving images at a rate of 20 frames per second.

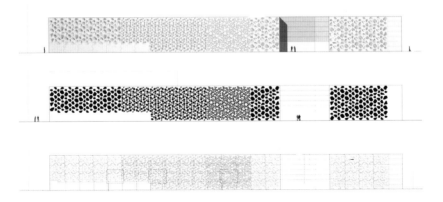

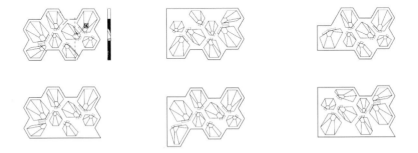

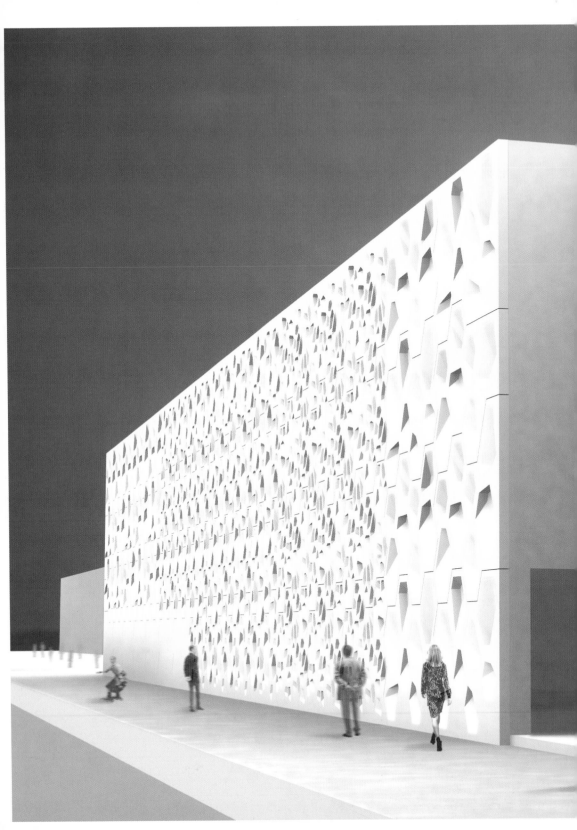

TEXTURE

The ideal illumination should enable us to appreciate the textures of materials. Light emphasizes the tectonic qualities of building materials. A brick or stone wall, depending on the illumination, can become an interesting feature in a room or a dark and boring separation. This is an important fact to keep in mind, so, in any project, the investment in materials and illumination should be well balanced. For example, a top quality, expensive green marble wall will result completely lifeless if it is not contemplated in a light which stresses its patterns and colours.

In the words of the Japanese illumination specialist, Kaoru Mende, to design illumination is to design shadows. This is particularly true when the desired effect is the enhancement of the textures of the materials. Excess light tends to flatten details and embossed features of buildings. In the illumination of facades, a moderate light and a careful study of the angles of illumination will provide better results than an uncontrolled energy waste. In order to highlight the volumes and make them stand out, it is advisable that the light shines from various directions without coinciding with the main angle of vision. Illuminating a building partially from certain angles can give buildings an air of mystery.

In contemporary architecture, illumination is not only used to enhance the qualities of other materials but it is beginning to exploit its own potential in creating textures. The type of luminaires, the installation and the composition of the light sources help create a luminous texture. Sometimes the light source itself can seem direct and aggressive, for example when fluorescent lights and LEDs are not concealed.

The Berlin studio Realties:United has worked this concept in some of their creations, such as the interior design carried out in the Kunsthaus in Graz, built by architect Peter Cook, where a multitude of circular fluorescent lights, fitted to the ceiling, illuminates the hall.

Sometimes the layout of luminaires may result in a "pattern." The possibilities are endless – polka dots, lineal, patterned, etc. The luminous texture can enhance the characteristics of a space. In some cases, these luminous textures can resemble artistic installations. An interesting example can be seen in the Aomori Art Museum in Japan, designed by Jun Aoki.

In addition to the traditional light sources (such as fluorescent and incandescent light bulbs), LED lighting, fibre optic lighting and LED panel lighting (small flat flexible screens), have been introduced on the market.

All these elements multiply the possibilities of creating new luminous textures. Even though the installation costs of this type of light sources may be high, this has to be set against lower maintenance costs (long life of the sources), and less energy waste in the long term. Low energy consumption light sources are recommendable. It is important to expect a certain upkeep of these "luminous textures" and to regulate their intensity to prevent annoyance among users and neighbours.

AOMORI MUSEUM OF ART

Architect: Jun Aoki & Associates
Location: Aomori city, Japan
Year: 2002
Sqm: 129 536

Aomori Museum of Art is the museum made up of a structure that is flat on top and uneven on the bottom and overlaid on an earthen landscape crisscrossed with trenches.

In addition to white cubical galleries inside the structure, there are interstitial spaces of different scales and proportions between the structure and the earth that serve as site-specific galleries. Parts of trenches that do not mesh with the structure are used as open-air galleries and work yards.

The exterior wall is a brick curtain wall, but the joints that come with a curtain wall are concealed by having the exterior wall as a whole absorb any displacement. As a result, the building looks like a brick-construction structure floating in the air. The trenches in the ground serve to relate the museum to the important Sannai Maruyama archeological site on nearby land.

At night, the main facade seems to let the light flow out through a delicate lattice-like wall. However, looking a little closer, it becomes apparent there is no such lattice – the facade is actually covered with small fluorescent arrows.

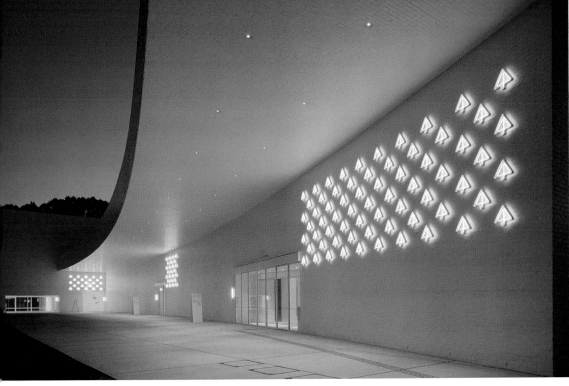

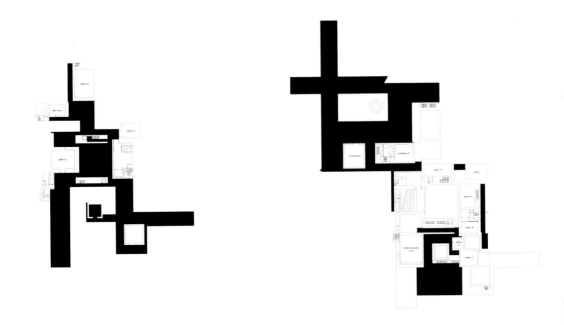

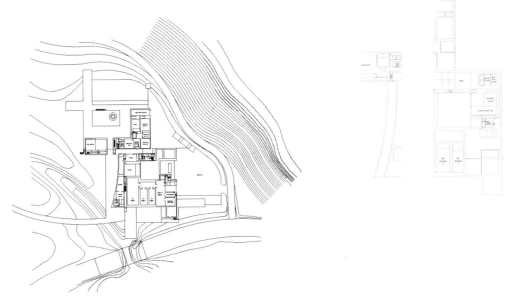

1F

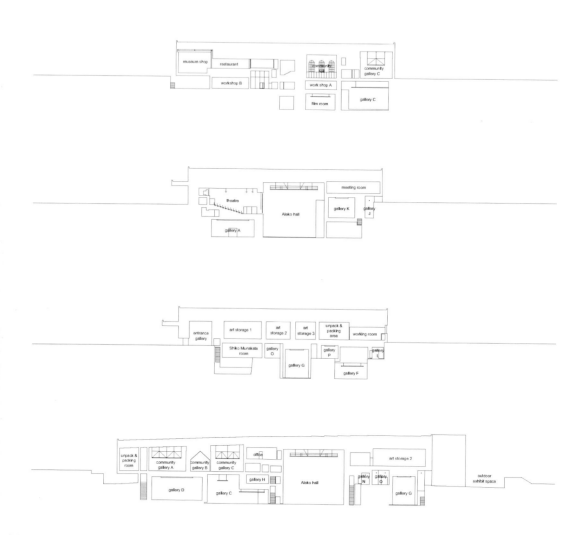

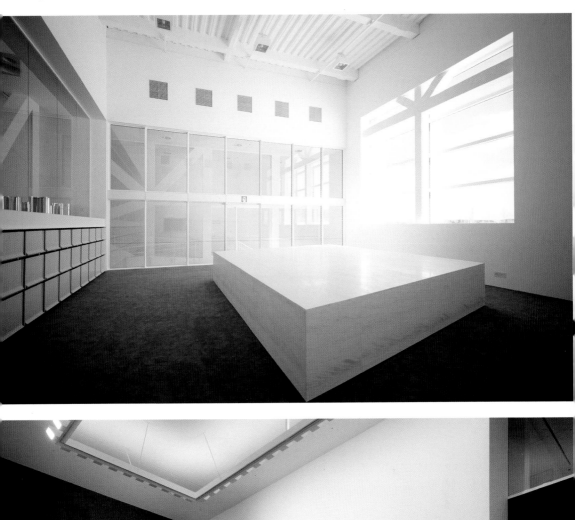

MUCEM MUSEE DES CIVILISATIONS DE L'EUROPE ET DE LA MEDITERRANEE

Architect: Rudy Ricciotti

Architect in charge of the project: Frédérique Pyra

Location: Marseille, France

Year: under construction - 2009

Sqm: 15 155

A boldly-drawn urban project sets out the doctrinal lines within which this project must forge its identity. First, a perfect square with a 72-metre side recalls the classic Latin, Greek or Oriental ground plan, under Pythagorean governance. Inscribed in this outer shape is another square with a 52-metre side, containing the exhibition halls and lecture rooms identifiable as the museum's core. Around, above and below are service spaces. Between the core and the service spaces, however, empty spaces circumscribe the central square, forming connecting areas, threaded as it were by old city lanes.

The visitor, in quest of the cultural, and with eyes drawn rather to the Fort, the sea or the port, will be naturally led this way. A route reminiscent of the tower of Babel or a ziggurat, with two intertwining ramps, leads the visitor upwards to the roof, looking out on the beckoning Fort St. Jean. The tectonic solution of building with an innovative, high-grade concrete derived from the latest research by the French industry reduces the impact of the material to the unobtrusive dimensions of skin and bone, thus asserting a mineral signature echoing the towering ramparts of the Fort St. Jean. A single material with a muted, light-flattened, dusty hue abstracts the beholder from the flashy vistas of technology-suffused consumerism, asserting instead the supremacy of denseness and fragility.

Mucem will be self-confessedly evanescent in its stone setting and Orient-leaning by the shadows that mark its
. By contrast, on the seaward side of the inlet, level with the pontoon, a glancing light over the blue water shot
silver shafts will assert the closeness of this piece of land to the ever-present sea.

TEXTURE

LOUIS VUITTON NAGOYA

Architect: Jun Aoki & Associates

Interior design: Louis Vuitton Malletier

Location: Nagoya city, Aichi Pref., Japan

Year: 1999

Sqm: 457

The exterior wall of Louis Vuitton Nagoya is composed of two layers: a layer of glass with a checkerboard pattern in which white and transparent squares alternate is on the outside, and a wall with a checkerboard pattern in which white and dark brown squares alternate is on the inside. The superimposition of the two patterns creates a third pattern. This third pattern does not actually exist, but we see it nevertheless. As proof that it does not actually exist, the pattern moves as we walk past the building. If we approach the building, the pattern becomes smaller in size.

The outer skin of the building has been made into something more phenomenal than material in character. It is an attempt to see to what extent the characteristics of a volume that do not depend on a container to give it form can be expressed in the actual world.

Detail of the vynil textu

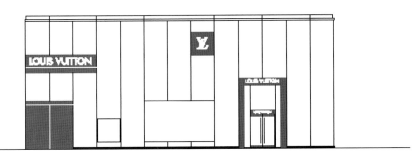

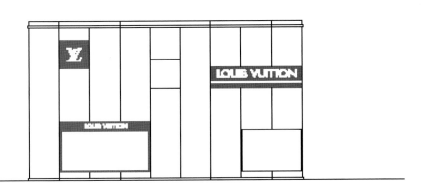

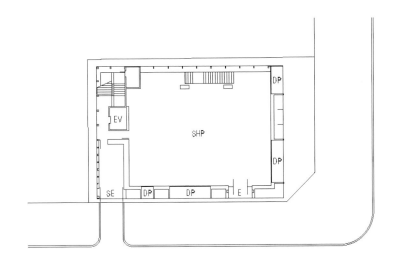

PROJECTION SURFACES

Perhaps some of the images that have most inspired media facades have their origins in the world of cinema and comics. The science fiction film *Blade Runner* by Ridley Scott (1982) is set in a dark and orientalised Los Angeles where towering skyscrapers are covered with adverts and moving images. This cult work goes forward in time and is also prophetic in regards to architecture, demonstrating the impact of the media-facades and a megalopolis which resembles some of today's Asian cities.

Today, the principal use of media-facades is for advertising and cultural purposes. It is proven that a moving image attracts the attention of possible consumers quicker than a static billboard. A good example of this is the facade for the T-mobil offices in Bonn, projected by the architects ag4, which look likes a screen from the street. From the interior, the facade is actually notably transparent, so that the activities of the users inside are not affected. This facade develops the concept of media-mesh and metallic meshes, normally made of stainless steel, joined to LED networks. When images are emitted these luminous points behave like the pixels of a computer screen or television. Another advantage of this system is that it adapts to any kind of shape without having to limit itself to flat surfaces, further expanding their innovative possibilities.

There are also buildings which incorporate luminous artistic installations on their exterior in place of advertisements. The installation Spots, created by the designers Realties: United, surprised pedestrians in the Potsdamer Platz in Berlin for 18 months by emitting videos created by different artists especially for this purpose, on the facade of an office building. The luminous system, made up of a matrix of 1800 small conventional fluorescent lamps, was at this time one of the largest media-facades in the world, although it was in black and white.

Another work by the Realities: United collective with a more permanent character is BIX, where they collaborated on the creation of the luminous exterior layer of the Kunsthaus of Graz, a building designed by Peter Cook. This "blob" shaped contemporary art museum is in strong contrast with its conventional setting. In this case, a matrix of fluorescent circles (930 units) was fitted onto the facade which is protected by a layer of transparent acrylic panels. Works by artists John le Kron and Carsten Nicolai have been projected there.

In other buildings, the facade does not act as a light emitting object, but as a screen for projections, just like in the classic outdoor cinemas. The Trevision factory, designed by the Austrian architects Queerkraft, shows images of relaxing alpine landscapes which are projected onto its facades. These images soften the impact of the factory within its environment. Another very attractive example is the projection of images by artist Tony Oursler, onto the facade of the AC hotel in Barcelona, projected by MAP architects. This temporal installation gives a phantasmagorical and intriguing air to the building. The projection of images or videos is often used in interior spaces, particularly in bars and clubs which search for dynamic and stimulating atmospheres.

Media-facades have a wide range of new possibilities. Installed in operas and auditoriums, they may enable a greater number of people to enjoy the shows. In many museums and other public buildings, they can provide users with information on exhibitions and activities held inside, creating a nexus between its content and the building itself. Preventing the abuse of these kind of facades is also important, as they can become quite aggressive and stressful for the passers-by. It is interesting to think about the effects this type of dynamic facade may have on the future of architectural composition, a field in which work is done traditionally in static terms.

MEDIA FACADE T-MOBILE

Architect: Prof. Peter Schmitz

Mediatecture: ag4 media facade Gmbh

Location: T-Mobile Headquarter, Bonn, Germany

Year: 2004

Sqm: 300

T-Mobile expanded its headquarters in Bonn in 2003. The result is a central building with a dual function as a forum for events and as a main entrance with reception lobby. T-Mobile was looking for a special kind of staging for its campus. It ideally should present the company logo on the front of the main building in an innovative way.

Ag4 built the world's first transparent media-facade for T-Mobile. It is a horizontal panel construction covering 300 square metres which is attached to the actual glass facade. The panels have integrated LEDs, ensuring the building displays full media capabilities. The distances between the single panels provide a clear view of the campus from the inside. The view from the square reveals the inner space superimposed by the electronic image. The transparency which can be perceived from both the inside and the outside is responsible for the special kind of magic of the transparent media-facade. The potential of the transparent media-facade has surpassed T-Mobile's greatest expectations; not only does the facade animate the company's logo, but the entire brand is staged by means of moving images and videos.

The basic display on the facade is a real-time self-generating programme which plays with the architecture of the T-Mobile building and the company's CI. The basic display is complemented by single, event-related sequences which can be animated, auto-active films that draw the viewer's attention to current events on the T-Mobile Campus.

The square in front of the media-facade of the T-Mobile Campus turns into an interactive playground. A camera records the movements on the square which are directly incorporated into the display of the media-facade. This makes it feasible to have a joint video game during lunch break; two players standing on the square can control their digital racquets on the media-facade with which they play a ball back and forth. It is even possible to display personal images via mobile phone or the Internet, in an edited version, on the facade.

SPOTS LIGHT

Architect: realities:united architects, Jan Edler and Tim Edler GbR

Location: Berlin, Germany

Year: 2006

Installation facade area: approx 1 350

Buildings communicate through their architecture and, as part of the architectonic concept, via their facades. In an age defined by the high-tech, architects also are increasingly making use of the latest communications technology in order to present their buildings on the public stage. Whereas a glass facade merely makes a building more transparent, the media-facade goes a step further. The dynamic surfaces – presentation areas for designs, animations or film sequences – turn the exterior shell of a building into a communication medium, an intermediary between structure and outdoor space. SPOTS, on show at Potsdamer Platz 10, is currently one of the world's largest media-facades. For a period of eighteen months, the eleven-storey glazed main facade of this office building owned by HVB Immobilien AG will host the light and media art installation SPOTS.

SPOTS comprises a light matrix of some 1,800 ordinary fluorescent lamps that is integrated into the ventilated glass facade of the building at Potsdamer Platz 10. A central computer linked to a bus system can control all of the lamps individually, adjusting their brightness or switching them on and off. As a result, designs, graphics and animation sequences can be recreated on the facade as moving luminous images. The external shell of the building is transformed into a communicative membrane, which will be used primarily for displaying artistic material. With its large grid pattern and low resolution, the matrix of fluorescent tubes harmonises with the architectural scales of the building and of Potsdamer Platz as a whole.

The entire concept of the SPOTS installation is aimed at integration into the architectonic system of the facade – with respect to technology, function and aesthetics. The impact of the installation is seen as an addition to the general communicative and intermediating function of the facade. This means that the content of the message conveyed by the commercial, 'prestigiously' designed building complex at Potsdamer Platz should be transferred to the system concept and also to the presentation concept.

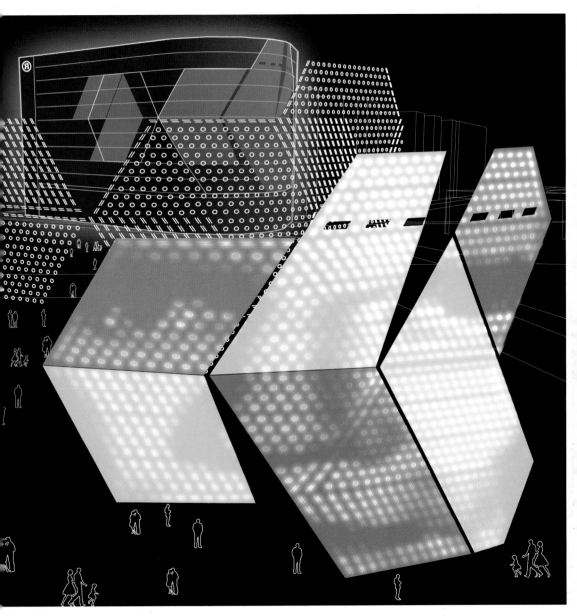

PROJECTION SURFACES

NOBEL PEACE CENTER

Architect: David Adjaye
Location: Oslo, Norway
Year: 2005
Sqm: 1 465

In this project different aspects of the Peace Prize programme are represented in a series of installations within a historic building, the old Vestbanen Station. The main interventions take the form of tubular elements which are used horizontally, to suggest movement, or vertically, to encourage visitors to pause. Within this strategy, materiality and light take on a key role at each stage.

The register is constructed of GRP and its inner walls are pierced by holes emitting the sounds of different languages and red or green light, representing places on the globe which are in conflict or at peace. The 8m-long volume of the register directs visitors to the reception area where the red resin finish and multiple reflections represent conflict, or to the Café de la Paix, where the decorative scheme by painter Chris Ofili employs a palette of soft greens. In the Passage of Honour, the walls, ceiling and floor are clad in brass, reflecting a golden light to celebrate the work of the most recent Peace Prize laureate. The Nobel Field is conceived as a garden in which the work of each prize winner is presented on a movement-activated screen supported on a stem-like structure; the spatial enclosure is constructed of panels of backlit blue-tinted glass. The external canopy forms a visual link with City Hall where the Peace Prize is presented.

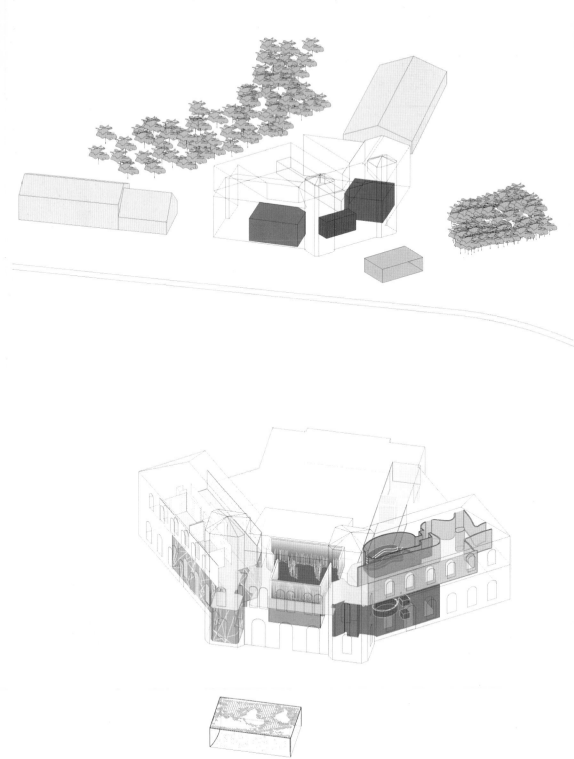

SENSITIVE FACADES

The sensitive facade can be defined as that which interacts with its surroundings. This concept thus includes many traditional systems. For example, the balcony doors of Mediterranean towns with their Venetian blinds of orientable slats, porticos, net curtains and lace curtains, provide a solution suitable for diverse conditions. Today, sensitive facades are those which, once built and/or programmed, do not depend on the user to adapt to the circumstances. They can be further classified into those sensitive to physical and meteorological conditions which surround a building, and those which respond to social, cultural and advertising stimuli, normally controlled by computer programs.

The aim of the first type of facade is most often to improve the heat and light conditions of buildings to generate energy savings. Although the cost of construction could be greater, the possible increase in the price of electric energy means increased demand for these kinds of facades. Investigation within the glass industry has led to the creation of many products with this purpose in mind, such as solar reflective glass, protective shielding glass, double glass with an acrylic chamber to redirect the light, etc.

Some facades work in very sophisticated ways in order to prevent the excessive warming up of interior spaces, such as the library of the Free University in Berlin, designed by Norman Foster. This sizeable domed space incorporates ideas from the concept of tensegrity and from the Climatroffice theory which Foster and Buckminster Fuller developed in the seventies. The structure of the dome is covered with a second skin which is separated from the first to create ventilation when the main body heats up excessively. The savings made in air conditioning can be up to 35 percent.

In other situations, the reason for these types of facades is to create visually poetic effects, such as is the case of the famous Wind Tower by Toyo Ito (Yokohama 1986).

The lighting system is controlled by computer programmes and sensors which modify the intensity and direction of various light sources on the basis of the wind's direction and speed, as well as the external noise. Another renowned example, also created in the eighties, is the photosensitive facade which the architect Jean Nouvel developed for the Institut du Monde Arabe (Paris 1987). Its lattice-like metal panels made up of diaphragms, which open and close depending on the light that is received, evoke the Arab aesthetic and decorative arts.

Among the sensitive facades which do not respond to their surrounding natural elements, there are those which aim to interact with visitors or to attract the attention of passers-by. Architects ag4 propose a kind of media and "participative" facade, where the images can be modified by mobile phone from the street. Corporations and public buildings are ever more innovative in using various "scenes" or light shows able to adapt depending on the occasion. For example, the Agbar Tower, designed by Jean Nouvel and B720 in Barcelona, uses different lighting programmes for different events, like those for New Year or football championships. The use of these attractive illuminations is to entertain and to achieve certain urban prominence. Public and private organisations use daring light compositions in the city centers to achieve popularity and recognition. As mentioned above, it is important to take into account the problem of light pollution and the danger of saturating the population with brightness and images, which is counter productive to the objectives of these organisations.

The sensitive facade is, however, an element which has still many possibilities to be explored and whose innovations will help in the construction of comfortable and beautiful buildings. As the architect Toyo Ito states, "I consider that the combination of primitive natural space and electronic technology will make tomorrow´s utopia in architecture."

FREE UNIVERSITY

Architect: Foster and Partners
Location: Berlin, Germany
Year: 2004
Sqm: 46 200

Since the end of World War II the Free University has occupied a central role in the intellectual life of Berlin. Today, with more than 60,000 students, it is the largest of Berlin's three universities. This redevelopment scheme includes the restoration of its Modernist buildings and the design of a new library on the campus.

The University's web-like campus was designed in 1963 by the architects Candilis Josic Woods Schiedhelm and the first buildings were completed in 1973. The facade, designed by Jean Prouvé, followed Le Corbusier's Modulor proportional system and consisted of framed panels in Corten steel which has self-protecting corrosive qualities.

As part of a comprehensive process of renovation the steel panels and framing have been replaced with patinated bronze elements.

Six of the University's courtyards have been united to form the site of a new library for the Faculty of Philology. The five-storey building is housed within a free-form skin consisting of aluminium panels, ventilation elements and double-layered glass panels, supported on steel frames with radial geometry. The library's curved form and its double skin create pressure differentials in the cavity between the skins, which assists a natural ventilation system. An inner membrane of glass fibre allows soft sunlight to penetrate the space while creating an atmosphere of concentration. Scattered transparent openings punctuate this membrane at strategic points to allow glimpses of the courtyard.

Some details have been sensitively altered to meet contemporary technical requirements and energy standards. The roof is covered with vegetation to add insulation and improve microclimatic conditions.

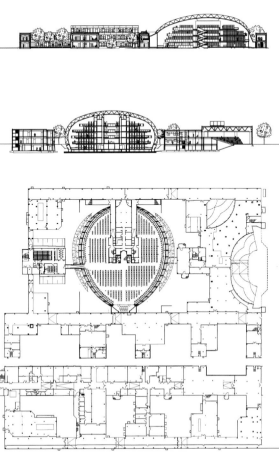

GALLERIA DEPARTMENT STORE

Architect: Un Studio
Location: Seoul, South Korea
Year: 2005
Sqm: Interior 21 986 / Facade 3 278

The Galleria Department Store project had two main goals. The first was a new facade that projects a lively, ever-changing surface. In total 4330 glass discs are mounted on the existing concrete skin of the building. The glass discs include special dicroic foil generating a mother-of-pearl effect during the day, while during the night each glass disc is lit by LED lights which can be programmed to create a multitude of effects. During the day the atmospheric and weather changes influence the degree of reflection and absorption of light and color on the glass circles, so that from different viewing points the appearance of each disc and the total surface changes constantly according to those external conditions that are beyond human control. During the night the lighting design developed for the facade additionally starts to interact with the material condition of the glass discs. By placing behind each of the glass discs an LED-light source and by controlling the lights digitally one by one, the possibilities to manipulate color and light emission become endless.

The second goal was the renovation of the interior into a luxurious integrated design. Inspired by the catwalk the customer finds himself immersed in the world of fashion while moving through the generous corridors. The illumination of the corridor is designed as a continuous lighting element, which consists of a linear rail following the direction of the corridors and bending whenever there is a change in direction. The interior design focuses on the elimination of superfluous details and introduces new integrated larger details.

AGBAR TOWER

Architect: Jean Nouvel
Lighting artist: Yann Kersalé
Location: Barcelona, Spain
Year: 2005
Sqm: 47 500

This is not a tower. It is not a skyscraper in the American sense of the expression; it is a unique growth in the middle of this rather calm city. But it is not the slender, nervous verticality of the spires and bell towers that often punctuate horizontal cities. Instead, it is a fluid mass that has perforated the ground – a geyser under a permanent calculated pressure.

The surface of this construction evokes the water; smooth and continuous but also vibrating and transparent because it manifests itself in coloured depths, uncertain, luminous and nuanced. This architecture comes from the earth but does not have the weight of stone. It could even be the faraway echo of old formal Catalan obsessions, carried by a mysterious wind from the coast of Montserrat.

The uncertainties of matter and light make the campanile of Agbar vibrate in the skyline of Barcelona - a faraway mirage day and night, a precise marker to the entry of the new diagonale that starts at Plaça de las Glorias. This singular object becomes a new symbol for an international city.

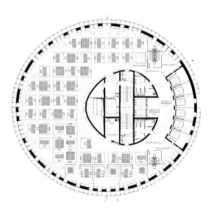

BIX PROJECT

Architect: realities:united architects - Jan Edler and Tim Edler
Location: Graz, Austria
Year: 2003
Sqm: 900

BIX is a matrix of 930 conventional fluorescent lamps integrated into the Plexiglas facade on the east side of the Kunsthaus. By regulating lamp brightness individually and over a continuous range at a frequency of 20 frames per second, it is possible to display images, films and animations in low resolution.

The BIX concept was initiated and developed in summer 2001 by the Berlin-based architects "realities:united." BIX was created as an additional feature of the Kunsthaus Graz at a time when overall planning had already reached an advanced stage. In addition to the late date and technical complexity of the project, it was also a challenge to integrate an architectural concept of foreign authorship into such an expressive building design. After all, BIX was a new design element that would dominate the structure's whole riverside frontage and call for a reinterpretation of the building's external hull or "skin."

Together the BIX media installation and the architecture of Kunsthaus Graz form a strong symbiotic relationship. The facade as a display screen expands the building's range of influence by bestowing the Kunsthaus with a communicative external appearance that complements its programmatically formulated communicative purpose. The media facade projects the internal processes of the Kunsthaus in an abstract and mediated form to the public. BIX acts as an architectural "enabler" and offers the Kunsthaus significantly more than just a spectacular presentational touch.

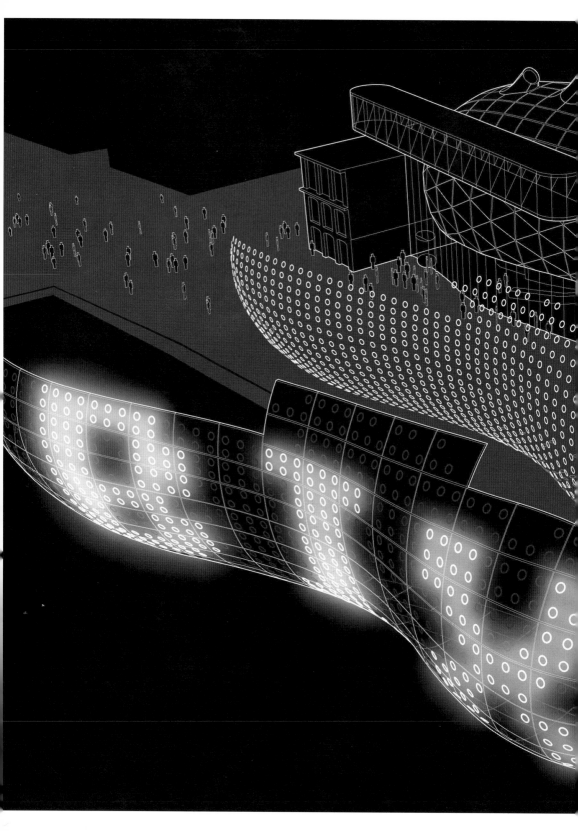

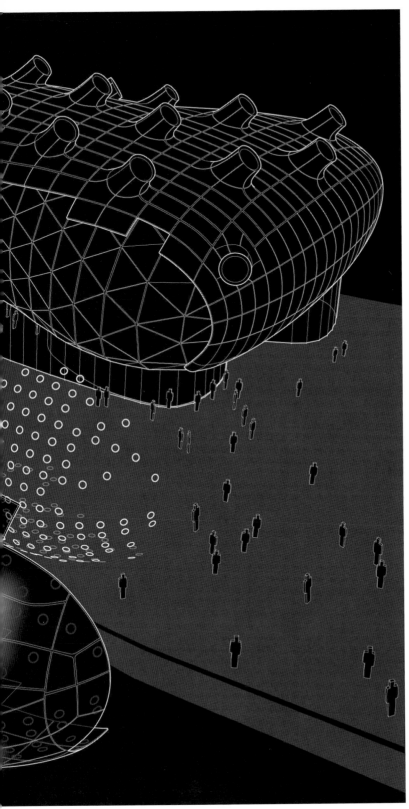

One has the impression that the blue bubble creates light patterns from within. Since the individual light sources are only visible when activated, the luminous signs appear as "tattooed" spots of pigment dancing freely on the structure's outer skin.

succeeds in highly inte-
ting picture and structure
ce there is no projection
een mounted in front of the
ding; instead the Kunst-
us itself radiates characters
images.

ERCO P3

Architect: Schneider and Schumacher
Lighting Design: Belzner Holmes
Location: Lüdenscheid, Germany
Year: 2002
Sqm: 3 365

Glowing blue-green in the dark, the ERCO's P3 automated warehouse facade reveals the internal processes of the crystalline building. Vertical lines continually form new patterns as they appear and disappear, group and regroup. Like shooting stars in the depth of the building the rack feeders can be seen as an amber glow on their ever busy permanently altering diagonal paths, more or less veiled by the stacked goods inside. This composition of light on the facades tells the story of the internal processes of the logistic machine, whereas inside one can actually see the logistic process of the machines. Content, casing and light are combined into one.

The changing patterns of light mirror the role of the computer controlled automated warehouse within the network of logistics. The light scenes interpret the following themes in moving, graphic images: transition between chaos and order, stacking, rearranging and optimizing. At the same time, the linear patterns also mimic the aesthetics of the ubiquitous barcodes, which identify goods and parcels. Special, amber-coloured LED panels display the movements of the rack feeders through the glass skin. Beyond the artistic interpretation there is no other light needed.

Behind the media-facade, a lighting control system dims and switches over 250 different light scenes. A total of 140 luminaires, each fitted with two fluorescent lamps and color filter sleeves in "special steel blue" reenact the internal drama. The fluorescent lamps are equipped with dimmable, electronic control gear and are joined together in 140 dimmer circuits.

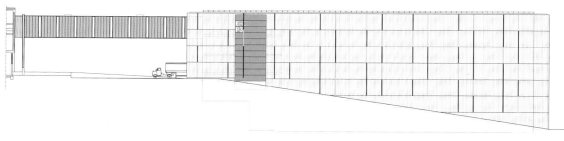

The drama of light and lines is visible for miles around and transforms the transparent construction into a sculpture of light.

COLOURED LIGHT

When studying the relationship between illumination and colour, the effect of natural or artificial light reflected on a given coloured surface should be distinguished from the characteristics of the light itself: its colour, frequency and temperature.

Colour is not an intrinsic physical property of objects but the result of a complex interaction between light radiation, the object's surface, the human eye and the perceptive capability of the observer. Visible light waves have a characteristic frequency which situates them in a particular strip of the electromagnetic spectrum – between 380 and 760nm. Within this area different coloured rays appear in the following order – violet, blue, green, yellow, orange and red. White light is a combination of all these colours. A light source will have a certain colour temperature which also depends on its thermal temperature. Oddly, sources with a lower colour temperature, such as candles (2000k) and incandescent light bulbs (3000k) create a warmer ambience than other light sources with higher colour temperatures, such as fluorescents (between 4000k and 5000k). Colour temperature can be measured objectively, however, and a light source's ability to reproduce colours is far more subjective and difficult to determine. The colour rendering index (CRI) has been developed to provide guidance in this complex field. In interior design, the colour and texture of every surface should be studied together with the chosen illumination, given that the overall effect may result very differently depending on the tonality and quality of reproduction of the light.

When a ray of light illuminates a surface, some of the radiation is absorbed and some is reflected. For example, when natural light illuminates a red object its surface reflects the red coloured rays and absorbs the remaining frequencies. The physiology of the observer is also a key factor in colour perception. Cells known as rods and cones in the retina transform the light radiation into electrical impulses which are then sent to the brain by optical nerves. It is here where the process which allows us to see different colours culminates. It has been proven that colour vision differs greatly among animal species; birds, reptiles and mammals all have a different sensitivity to colour. Nocturnal animals only see in black and white and humans who suffer from colour blindness are unable to distinguish colours correctly.

There are two groups of primary colours - the additive primaries and the subtractive primaries. The former consists of red, green and blue and can generate all the other colours by a combination of lights. This system called RGB is used in televisions and computer screens. The intersection of the three rays of light produces white light. The subtractive primaries are those used in the mixing of paints and ink for printing and are magenta, cyan and yellow.

Coloured lighting is traditionally used on theatre sets, in shows and in concerts. Interior designers also use it in night clubs and bars. Starting in the sixties, several artists, such as James Turrel and Dan Flavin developed studies on the effect of coloured light on space which have greatly influenced contemporary architecture. Today the use of coloured lights is ever more common in all types of buildings, given that architects, interior designers and lighting experts have learned to appreciate the ability of colour to alter people's moods and radically modify the interior and exterior aspect of buildings.

COLOURED LIGHT

CASTELL ZUOZ

Architect: Un Studio
Location: Herrliberg, Switzerland
Year: 2004
Sqm: 24 240

The Hotel Castell in Zuoz is spectacularly situated offering stunning views of the Engadin valley. In the hotel's second phase of rigorous modernization Un Studio has designed a new apartment building with 14 luxury dwellings, newly designed half of the rooms in the existing hotel and extensively renovated the basement. In the remodeling of the historic hotel's basement the traditional hamam design has been reinterpreted creating an atmosphere of quiet contemplation. Areas of movement and rest are arranged fluently around cylindrical rooms washed with different coloured lights.

Spectacularly situated at 1900 m altitude with a view of the neighboring resort of St. Moritz, the newly constructed transparent, restrained volume stands next to the main structure of the hotel, which dates from 1912.

The Bar Rouge in the hotel, designed by multimedia artist Pipilotti Rist and the Zurich architect Gabrielle Hächler, exemplifies the ambitions of the owners. This sensuous bar rises up boldly like a large, curved, avant-garde question mark.

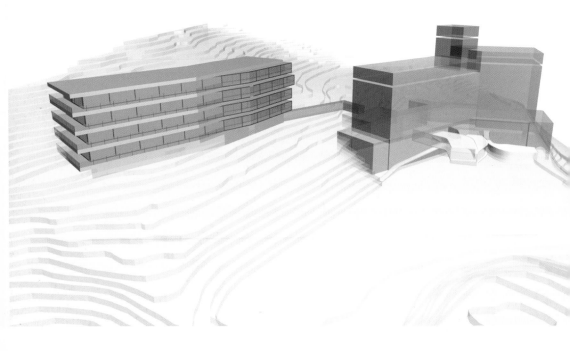

COLOURED LIGHT

GUARDERIA ELS COLORS

Architect: RCR Rafael Aranda. Carme Pigem. Ramón Vilalta Arquitectes
Location: Manlleu, Spain
Year: 2004
Sqm: 927

When playing with a child's wooden piece set, one can obtain varied compositions which, transferred to the field of architecture, somehow match the distribution of volumes and spaces during the creation process of a building. Each one of the colours covers a different volume, in such a way that it is possible to keep identifying them as autonomous pieces even when they become part of the whole. Colour is the best device when it comes to defining and recognizing independent prisms. These chromatic variations and also the incorporation of the perspective of children and their capacity to grasp the exterior world were the guidelines in the design of this kindergarten in Manlleu, Barcelona.

The chosen plot lies across the street that surrounds the cemetery, so there is a wide open space in front of it. The opposite street stretches all the way to the Ter River. Between them, the kindergarten unfolds over an orthogonal grid consisting of eight rectangular prisms distributed in two bands that house the shared spaces in their first volumes and the classrooms in the consecutive ones, all crossed by a ninth elongated piece that lies transversal to both rows and links them as a sort of porch.

The spaces for children have one height only (their perspective, from bottom to top, broadens their relative perception, something that has been kept in mind during the design of the center) and only the teachers' lounge and the principal's offices are in the upper level.

.

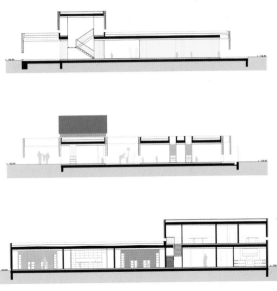

COLOURED LIGHT

CASA SACERDOTAL
DIOCESANA DE PLASENCIA

Architect: Andrés Jaque Arquitectos
Location: Plasencia, Spain
Year: 2004
Sqm: 4 055

The priestly house appears as an infrastructure that needs modification. The chapel is a transformable space, open to creative configurations of its users. The sacristy is not a closed and opaque room, but rather diluted in a series of accessible showcase-cupboards accessible from the place of celebration. Part of the garden is parcelled to promote recreational cultivation by means of individual assignments. Also there are elements where personal decision is possible: garden lights with a switch, a front of aviaries for the care of pets and moveable bonfire-lamps.

The exterior surfaces, the facades, are active spaces of communication with immediate procedures; light boxes available for internal announcements, a slate patio area with a blackboard as a medium for chalk messages and coloured lights with individual switches in the rooms thus create a changing code over the skyline of the city.

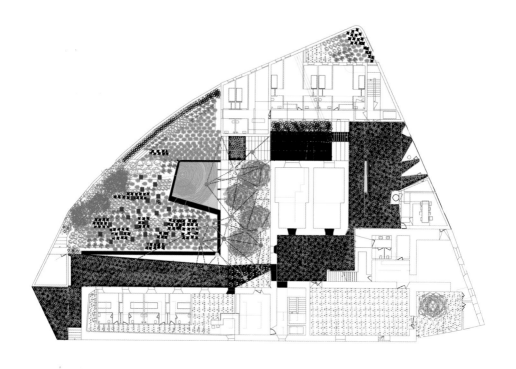

COLOURED LIGHT

MARSTALL MENSA

Architect: Schroder Stichs Volkman
Lighting design: Belzner Holmes
Location: Heidelberg, Germany
Year: 2003

The building was built over 500 years ago. In 2001 after a long period of relative neglect, the building was to be reactivated as a student canteen open at night to serve dinner until late and as a lounge, not only catering to students, but also to faculty members and visiting tourists.

Light from the beginning would play a supporting role and in some places be a major design element. It was also conceived as dynamic light composition that presents itself in very different manners according to the desired atmosphere as a functional coffeehouse during the day and as a lounge at night.

For the main lighting of the hall a dual system was designed. For the gothic segment, four flat luminaries hang from the ceiling creating a quiet but obvious new plane. These custom-made lights directly light the areas below always presenting the patrons below with a beneficial light while indirectly immersing the old shell in varying colours. Applying gradual shifts in colour per segment, the perception of the expansion of the space can be influenced.

All elements combined create a lighting instrument of high complexity. Playing or programming it takes much experience as small changes in colour or light level balances can easily dull or even destroy the spatial atmosphere. To ensure the standards, the bar operators are provided a choice of 12 cues or cue sequences so they can manually choose the light according to the internal use or external weather. The preset queues include: dark day, light day, three different lounge cues, concert, lecture, large screen video and so on.

The green coloured glass structure of the barfront is back-lit by a dynamic blue to green light. Seemingly random light strips are integrated under the galleries illuminating the bar and the bartenders, while the reflected light underlights the gallery and lets it float in space.

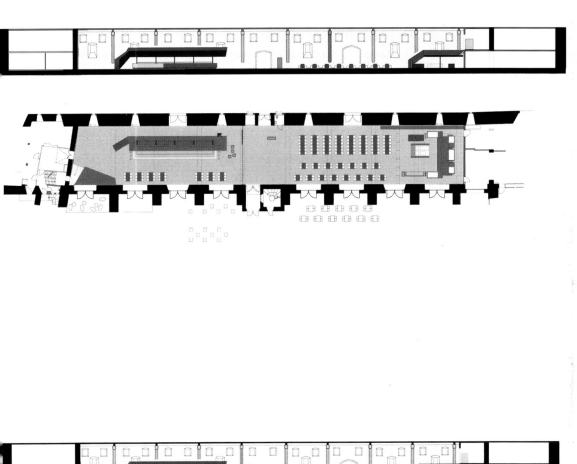

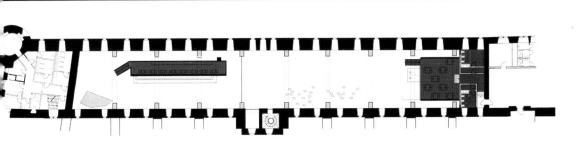

INDIRECT LIGHT

Indirect illumination occurs when a ray of light that has already been reflected onto a surface is diffused into a space. It produces a smooth and dispersed light without excessive contrasts - ideal for preventing dazzling and visual fatigue. It reduces the harsh shadows created by spotlights, thus preventing the "dark corner" effect. By illuminating ceilings and walls, indirect light tends to visually enlarge spaces. It is the perfect illumination with which to create a relaxed ambience, such as for bedrooms, spas, bars, restaurants, lounge areas, etc. In a domestic or work setting this kind of lighting is normally combined with direct light or task-lighting where required. In most offices, indirect lighting has the advantage of minimizing the annoying glares on computer screens. The resulting light creates pleasant atmospheres and is usually more comfortable than direct luminaries with louvers (a system incorporated into lamps to avoid reflections). To complete the illumination, task-lights are recommended since indirect light is unsuitable for reading and detailed work.

With indirect illumination, light is usually directed towards the ceiling or walls. A lighting system based on surface reflection is uneconomical since light is dispersed and not concentrated where most needed. Indirect light will reach the work plane after having been reflected onto the walls and ceilings.This means their characteristics, colour, tone, material, etc., should be kept in mind. A light coloured ceiling will only reflect about 70-80 percent of the light it receives, while pale coloured walls will only reflect between 50-60 percent. Light lost through absorption should be included in the general estimation of illumination needed for a particular space. To truly maximise the intensity of indirect light, the walls and ceilings should be painted in white or in a very clear colour. It is also important to clean the light installations and luminaries regularly to maintain a stable level of light. Indirect illumination is not suitable for precision work given that it makes three dimensional objects appear flat because of the absence of shadows.

This type of soft ambient illumination is ideal for relaxing atmospheres and also for passing spaces, such as corridors and passages. A large part of the London Underground is lit up this way. Indirect lighting lamps were the height of fashion in the 1920's and 1930's, especially during the Art Deco movement, when they were very common in hotels and restaurants.

It would be true to say that indirect light as an illumination base is highly recommendable since it enhances the characteristics of a space in a pleasant and simple manner. Often, additional lighting elements should be added to the base so the result is not boring or flat, two of this type of lighting's disadvantages, according to its detractors.

INDIRECT LIGHT

51 EINFAMILIENHAUS

Architect: Alles Wird Gut
Location: Wien, Austria
Year: 2003
Sqm: 456

This site in an exclusive residential area in the Viennese district of Hietzing includes a 1500 sqm private park and is situated 2.7 m above street level. Behind that wall, a partly covered entrance courtyard appears and a first view across the lobby shows a lowered garden. While the view ushers deeper into the house, the path changes direction, loops to the stairs and leads to the upper living area above the main garden level.

The "public" areas are conceived as folded level which form a continuous transition between the living spaces. The garden is implicated and the site adopts its shape. The areas at street level, actually subterranean, become living space with their own character due to cuttings in the landscape. The living areas on the garden level are extroverted and open up generously southbound to the garden in contrast to those situated in the lower part of the building. Partly covered and preliminary open terraces and pergola terraces blur the transition between interior and exterior room and form diverse situations, depending on mood or season. Small inner courtyards provide intimate outdoor spaces as well as additional light for the inner zones of the deep structure. Specially placed windows support the amazing view into the park and over the city of Vienna on its northern side.

The living areas offer a great variety of room situations by special organisation of room height, narrowing, perspective and view.

EXTERIOR LIGHTING

During the day, the main exterior light is sunlight, the brightest light on our planet. It's the most balanced in chromatic terms and it's brighter than any other light source invented by man. On a sunny day, exterior light can reach between 10,000 and 100,000 luxes (the standard DIN requires a level of 500 luxes for offices and other similar work spaces). It is not an even source of light since its qualities change immensely over the course of the day. Sunlight has a well defined daily cycle, which depends on the geographic setting and also on the day of the year and the season. The sun comes up, then rises slowly until it reaches the central point of its arc, and finally goes down until it disappears. The intensity of light, its direction and its colours change throughout the day, which is the time the earth needs to rotate around its axis. This constant variation connects us to the cosmic rhythm of the universe.

During the day, the exterior light also depends on the atmospheric conditions of the sky. The golden sunlight on a September evening is a world away from the cold steely light on a rainy winter's day. The sun's characteristics can be greatly affected by the environmental humidity, the clouds and the contamination.

At night, exterior lighting usually depends on artificial light. Then, the only natural light we can see is the one from the moon and the stars. Moonlight is actually the reflection of the sun on this satellite. Unfortunately it is becoming more and more difficult to enjoy the shining stars in urban areas or growing urbanizations. Excessive nocturne light, called light pollution, is a growing problem in built up areas. It not only means a useless waste of energy, but also a nuisance for people in their surroundings. It can also disorientate and harm the health of birds and other animals.

In spite of this problem, which occurs when the light is badly projected or used inappropriately, a good exterior artificial illumination is necessary and has many advantages. Apart from the obvious benefit of being able to see where one is going and driving, it brings vitality and life to the streets, squares, commercial and other urban areas. Nocturne illumination in parks and gardens allows the enjoyment of these places for longer hours, especially during the winter months. At night, when they are carefully illuminated, the appearance of these spaces changes radically, creating magical and mysterious atmospheres.

Another of its main advantages is real and perceived security. It has been demonstrated that an improvement in lighting in unsafe neighbourhoods has managed to reduce delinquency and vandalism levels.

Exterior lighting also has the capacity to bring a certain unity and order to an urban space. Light can create visual hierarchies and links, highlighting some areas or buildings and leaving chaotic or uninteresting spaces in darkness. A careful illumination of buildings and monuments prolongs the time to enjoy architecture and to sightsee. This is why studies of night time illumination are more and more frequent, where cities and whole regions or landscapes are involved. Subtlety and sensitivity as well as certain restraint are the best strategies in the conception of light design.

As mentioned earlier, this book is not a technical manual of lighting or a scientific analysis on the subject, but it focuses on the growing presence of lighting in contemporary architecture. It is one of many possible views of the unlimited relationship between light and architecture and how they interact together in today's architectural projects.

URBAN SPACES

The illumination of urban spaces is essential for obvious practical reasons. In Roman times, torches were used to light some of the principal pathways. Nocturnal illumination prolongs the use of urban spaces at night. It provides vision when nature alone cannot give enough light, making it possible to walk and drive along the streets. Urban illumination is also vital for keeping urban zones safe. In a well illuminated exterior space it is not only easier to detect dangerous situations earlier but these situations tend to occur less often. The effect of adequate lighting brings, psychologically, greater peace of mind and also creates a safer urban environment after night fall.

Today the function of urban illumination goes far beyond the creation of minimum conditions in order to go from one place to another. Light is one of the main tools used by planners to influence the ambience of a street and alter the mood of the passer-by. Decorating streets with Christmas lights is a good example of the way in which attractive lighting can provoke optimism and help activate commercial areas. Las Vegas is a paradigmatic case of how the use of light can be abused to incite consumption.

Good urban lighting, however, is not about excess or uncontrolled illumination with no concern for the characteristics of the space; in fact, it is the exact opposite. The application of an "illumination project" in the urban space can have very beneficial consequences for an area at night. As with any other architectural project, the setting, the characteristics of the place and the function the exterior space will assume are all aspects which will set the guidelines. Quality urban illumination should have ambition - a clear idea of what is to be expressed - as well as meeting the practical demands. It is also advisable to have a clear concept that keeps in mind the lighting design and serves as a guideline in specific decisions.

Just as the illumination specialist Hervé Descottes states, light has a social and a political dimension: "Light is associated with power and brings a sense of authority with its numerous privileges and inequalities." It creates hierarchies and spatial order in towns. Light has the capacity to indicate routes, enhance monuments and squares and also to mark priorities of some connections over others. When streets and lineal spaces are planned, light can indicate the main way for the passer-by: a well-lit street will almost always be chosen over a darker one. Darkness has the advantage of covering up that which is best not seen. It enables the most uneven characteristics and ugliest buildings to be concealed in order to enhance the most attractive aspects of a place. It is said, and with good reason, that a good lighting project can help save a bad urban project. This is particularly true when an urban space is deemed boring at night time.

The illumination of a public place has to be planned differently depending on whether the urban setting is a new creation or an already existing area. Generally, when the illumination is being designed for a new construction, the study of light is incorporated into the rest of the urban project whose main objectives will be to enhance specific zones in accordance with the urban plan. There should be close communication in such situations between the urban planners and the lighting specialists, hopefully generating interesting ideas on both parts and strengthening the total concept. When the lighting project involves a historic part of town or is in an existing urban environment, more factors need to be considered such as the main monuments, the historic remains, the most interesting facades, etc. The project should be sensitive to these elements and the lighting plan needs to be flexible in order to cater to the special illumination of certain features. The needs and wishes of shopkeepers and neighbours should not be overlooked since their opinions and ideas may be useful in responding to the requirements of the place.

It is necessary to know and understand the desired character of a street or walkway to achieve a successful illumination. A roundabout or a commercial street has very different characteristics from a quiet romantic side-street in the old town. The light intensity, the type of luminaries and the way light is directed all depend on the desired effect. Generally speaking, light inspires enthusiasm and dynamism. When searching for a relaxing ambience, lighting levels should be low, and, where possible, it is preferable to illuminate from lower than eye-level to avoid dazzling. A good example is the Jungfernsteig Square in Hamburg, created by the architects WES & Partner, which is illuminated by lights fitted into the benches and directed toward the ground. Sometimes an excess of light can destroy the picturesque ambience of an old quarter of town. The evocative images of towns such as Prague and Vienna are closely linked to the memory of their mysterious shadows. The lighting specialist must resolve the practical requirements and at the same time, act as a scenic director, creating compositions which are capable to silently move those who observe them.

Public space is by definition a shared space which will be used by different kinds of people with distinct tastes and sensitivities. This is why the design of urban lighting should be simple in most occasions. In general, due to its cost, urban lighting is not replaced often which means that eccentric ideas are not recommendable.

It is vital that urban fittings are durable, resistant to harsh weather and easy to maintain. In areas near the coast, like maritime promenades, the street lamps are particularly at risk of rusting so the correct choice of materials is paramount – cast iron and stainless steel being good options. It is often far more economical in the long term to invest in good quality urban luminaries rather than paying for the maintenance and reparation of inferior quality models over time. Public lighting should also be robust enough to withstand acts of vandalism.

A well-designed urban illumination must meet a great number of requirements. Streets should be comfortable places to walk by with a minimum amount of obstacles for pedestrians and free from architectural barriers. On narrow streets, this is something that must be considered in the choice of luminaries. In squares and in wide open spaces, it is quite common to fit several sources of light at different heights in one lighting pole to avoid cluttering the space. Another solution is to use a focus of light embedded in the pavement.

Saving energy is one of the main objectives in urban lighting design. This depends on the efficiency of the light source and also on the characteristics of the fitting itself. In order to prevent light contamination, urban luminaries should direct their light toward the ground, not the sky. A good lighting design is economical in the long term and prevents plenty of problems.

STREETS AND LINEAL SPACE

An adequate lighting system can help regenerate spaces and underused areas while improving the general aspect of the streets at night time. A good illumination project focuses on the quality of light and its effects on the urban space rather than only choosing an attractive model of lamp. Town councils and local authorities are beginning to appreciate the benefits that a good and interesting urban illumination can bring to citizens and visitors.

Lighting is without a doubt a very useful tool to promote commercial areas and to create a better ambiance at night in zones that are perceived as residual spaces. In the lighting design of a lineal space, it is important to be conscious of the dimensions and section of the street in order to choose the appropriate lights. The projection of the beam of the luminaries must be analysed to guarantee there are no inadequate dark zones in the street. One must calculate the number of street lights that are necessary and the recommendable distance between them.

Today, lighting proposals for whole neighbourhoods or towns are becoming more and more frequent. Sometimes lighting can help bring new life to former industrial spaces or to abandoned infrastructures.

STREETS AND LINEAL SPACE

NICCOLO PAGANINI AUDITORIUM

Architect: Renzo Piano Building Workshop
Location: Parma, Italy
Year: 2001
Sqm: 7 222

The conversion of a neglected 19th century industrial building into an auditorium is praised both for its acoustic qualities and the lightness and transparency of its renovation.

The Paganini Auditorium was built inside the unused Eridania sugar factory, a group of industrial buildings of extremely different volumes and structure types.

The project included eliminating the main body's transversal curtain walls and replacing them with three large glass walls to ensure transparency throughout the length of the 90 metres long building. Even during concerts, the park can be seen from any viewpoint in the hall and foyer. A system of soundproof panels hung from the trusses over the stage completes the spatial organisation of the main body.

The public enters through the south end and proceeds through the building's length: there is first a roofed open air space, leading inside and passing through the first wide glass wall, and from here one continues on to the two-level foyer.

e auditorium stands in the middle of a park like a huge transparent music box. This not only provides beneficial nditions for acoustical isolation, but also becomes an integral part of the design. Replacing the transverse curtain lls with three large glass walls ensures transparency throughout the length of the building and provides the audice with a scenic view of nature.

IN OUT SONY CENTER

Architect: Helmut Jahn

Lighting artist: Yann Kersalé

Location: Berlin, Germany

Year: 2001

Sqm: 3 500

Close to the Potsdamer Platz in Berlin, the Sony Center, built by Helmut Jahn was erected on a terrain that used to be a huge no man's land at the time of the Wall. The tower block occupied by office buildings, housing, and a hotel sourrounds an oval forum of 4000 square metres accommodating theatres, cinemas, restaurants, and bars.

The Forum, with its intense nightlife reminiscent of the Potsdamer Platz of the 1920's, is covered by a high dome made of glass sheets under which bands of diaphanous material forming a corolla are stretched out by a system of cables. Seen from the rest of the town, this cap, designed by the structural engineering firm Ove Arup + Partners, resembles a volcano. At the top, luminous sources shining downwards had been planned. The lighting of the Forum was conceived as something emanating from within, with apulsation expressing nocturnal life, both radiating light and sending signals. The only other undertaking was the positioning of blue neon lights at the angles of the buildings, accentuating the multiple entrances to the Forum and anchoring this huge jellyfish to the ground.

As soon as the restaurants and theatres open, the high marquee, white until dusk, starts to decline all the colours of the spectrum, from magenta to cyan, with the exception of yellow. When the Forum empties out, the dome turns into an intense blue, which, in the morning, fades back into white.

STREETS AND LINEAL SPACE

POWERPLANT ARTISTIC LIGHT INSTALLATION

Architect: realities:united in cooperation with Nik Hafermaas
Location: Pasadena - Los Angeles, USA
Year: under construction - 2008
Sqm: 700 000

The change from heavy industry to innovation-driven enterprises and institutions is reflective of Pasadena's identity as a city of learning at the forefront of new models of urban planning.

Any appropriate artistic solution must meet the goal of creating a significant symbolic gesture that is at once powerfully expressive of the ideas it represents and also in accord with community standards for aesthetic and environmental impact. PWP Power Plant site, located at the literal southern gateway to the city of Pasadena, provides a perfect environment for a transformative and ethereal art installation that achieves these goals.

Sprouting like artistically engineered seeds in the cracks of smokestack industry sidewalks, clusters of PowerPlants will reach skyward, suggesting the form of southern California's ubiquitous palm trees while embodying the substance of Pasadena's urban and social transformation. The slender steel or fiberglass structures (approximately 6" in diameter at the base) will vary in height — from 55 to 78 feet tall, depending on the exact location — and be topped with a clear acrylic free rotating illuminated bar that emits a warm lambent glow (only 30 watts). Each stalk will be freestanding, rising from a 6' deep foundation, and self-sustaining, powered by a discreet (2-3 sq. ft.) solar panel and an energy-storing rechargeable battery. That means each PowerPlant can be easily "planted" or "replanted" as necessary. Patterns of lighting, ranging from abstract configurations to a uniform glow, will be computer controlled through a wireless network. With a natural form that interacts with the environment — gently swaying in the breeze, the light bars indicating wind direction like celestial weather vanes — PowerPlants are completely appropriate to the site. They are symbolic of the city's role at the forefront of arts and culture and of the neighborhood's transition from traditional to innovative industry.

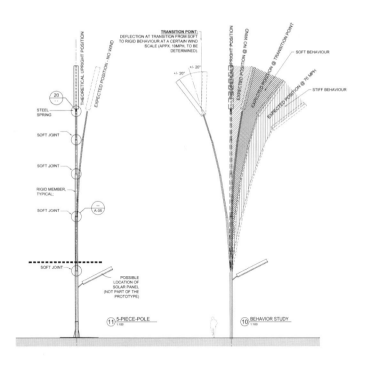

THEORETICAL UPRIGHT POSITION

EXPECTED POSITION - NO WIND

20

STEEL SPRING

SOFT JOINT

SOFT JOINT

RIGID MEMBER, TYPICAL;

SOFT JOINT

A-05

SOFT JOINT

POSSIBLE LOCATION OF SOLAR PANEL (NOT PART OF THE PROTOTYPE)

TRANSITION POINT:
DEFLECTION AT TRANSITION FROM SOFT TO RIGID BEHAVIOUR AT A CERTAIN WIND SCALE (APPX. 10MPH, TO BE DETERMINED).

+/- 20°   +/- 20°

THEORETICAL UPRIGHT POSITION

EXPECTED POSITION @ NO WIND

EXPECTED POSITION @ TRANSITION POINT

SOFT BEHAVIOUR

EXPECTED POSITION @ 70 MPH

STIFF BEHAVIOUR

11 5-PIECE-POLE
1:100

10 BEHAVIOR STUDY
1:100

SQUARES

In most towns and cities, squares represent areas of centrality and interaction in the urban structure. They are not only spaces to walk through, but also places to sit down, meet others, or play. This makes lighting projects for squares especially interesting and ambitious since the observers usually have the time to enjoy more sophisticated compositions. The trend today is to view the illumination of these places as something dynamic which varies and adapts to different circumstances. For example, different scenes can be programmed according to needs, composing more eye-catching and daring scenes on holidays and other more modest and simple scenes for other days. In more advanced programmes, light can vary continuously in a very subtle way, imitating natural light.

Most times, the architectural project for a square incorporates a lighting proposal. Technological advances in the field of light sources and control systems have greatly widened the creative possibilities, making it very recommendable to integrate a lighting specialist in the design team. For example, the introduction of LED lighting technologies has given greater importance and sophistication to the creative possibilities of light in urban spaces.

ELEFTHERIA SQUARE

Architect: Zaha Hadid and Patrik Schumacher
Location: Nicosia, Cyprus
Year: not realized yet
Sqm: 1 600

The concept takes the form of an architectural intervention, which is only one part of a much larger urban planning gesture that aspires to organise and synthesise the whole of the Venetian Wall, the moat and the fringes of the two parts of the city (inner and outer) into a unified whole.

The moat becomes a Green Belt which as a 'necklace' surrounds and unifies the Venetian Wall and can become Nicosia's Main Park, enhancing the quality of life by offering a range of recreational facilities such as spaces for rest during day time and for walking and exercise during the cooler hours of the evening. It can also be used for art exhibitions and installations, sculpture gardens and sports activities, all around the perimeter of the Venetian Walls.

In order to achieve this, they proposed a car traffic analysis to calculate the required capacity for car parking and consolidation in privately run car park facilities, which can be placed under the streets, such as the one proposed under Omirou Ave, and even partly under the garden surface of the moat. The placement of car parks under the garden surface would allow the "topographical inflations" to be combined with connections to the street level and maximize the available parking spaces making the construction of these projects feasible. The Venetian Wall would be restored and lit continuously to emphasise its presence during the night time. A pedestrian path lined with a continuous row of palm trees creates a walkway right next to the Wall.

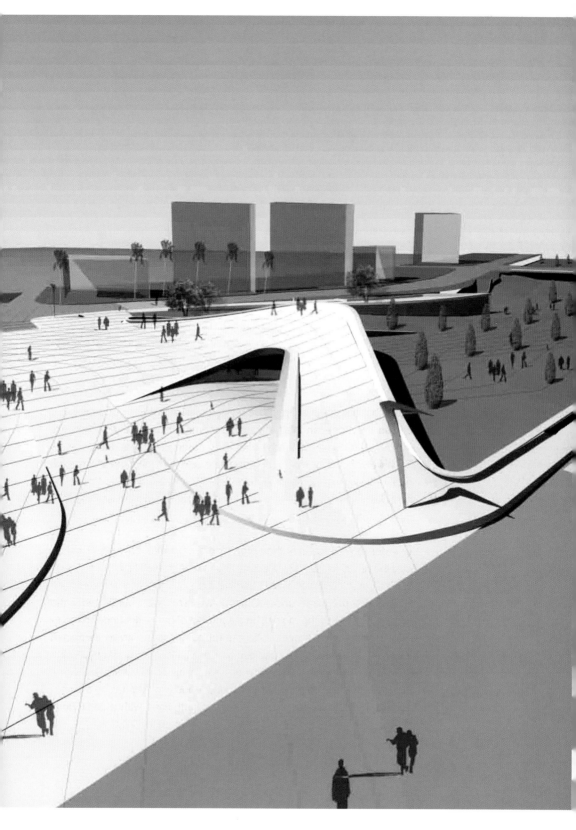

Eleftheria square and the other bridging streets to the outer perimeter of the Venetian Wall become the gates to the inner city, which could have restricted access to cars and more pedestrianised streets.

DALI SQUARE

Architect: Francisco José Mangado Beloqui
Location: Madrid, Spain
Year: 2005
Sqm: 23 090

Dali Square, otherwise known as Felipe II Avenue, is a complex space of great value in the urban network of the centre of Madrid. The architectural proposal holds a double and simultaneous interest. The improvement, repaving and restructuring of the complex aims to bestow on it a formal significance in harmony with its importance as a central public space in the city without overlooking the idea of a unitary image for the whole area.

The unit is greatly defined by the new pavement. It is a "dense" pavement, built in granite and cast bronze, which incorporates the sculptural essence elaborated by the sculptor Fransesc Torres, as well as the LED luminous lines which give the complex a new geometric order and visual richness. The pavement, which in this case is the sole instrument with urban transformation capacity, assumes a dimension which goes beyond the strictly material and secondary, and assumes a necessary conceptual and strategic value. The style of the enclosed spaces, of more playful and domestic dimensions, is created by gardened areas which rise and incline up from the pavement and have a sufficient depth of soil for plants and trees, and urban furniture and benches making it a more enjoyable space.

Light has been used creatively and gives constancy to the new "configuration." It has been used as a physical part of the pavement but also in the transformation of the entrances to the underground car park and pedestrian areas, which could not be changed. These have been converted into illuminated structures, whose size and situation give them importance, transforming them into active elements, formally assessed within the new urbanisation. They rise up from the ground, especially at night, like "minerals" in a further reference to the inexistent subsoil.

SQUARES

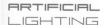
SQUARES

PEY BERLAND SQUARE

Architect: Francisco José Mangado Beloqui
In cooperation with King Kong 5

Location: Bordeaux, France

Year: 2003

Sqm: 30 000

The luminous ambience is the result of combining a general illumination with a peripheral illumination, using a soft and homogeneous light which becomes softer towards the centre of the square. The lighting of the Saint Andre Cathedral and the Pey-Berland tower brings the place to its zenith.

The general illumination is based on the facade. The luminous elements include: the luminous strips fitted into the ground which increase in frequency towards the centre of the square and the cathedral (see plans), the luminous posts set out in clusters and the lights fitted into the benches and into the structures of the kiosks and cark part exits.

The illumination furniture:
- Illumination posts / 3 "clusters" of three posts: situated near the kiosk, in front of the town hall and north of the main garden.
- Copper street lamps on cantilevers on the peripheral facades of the square.
- Copper furnished lanterns on console tables.

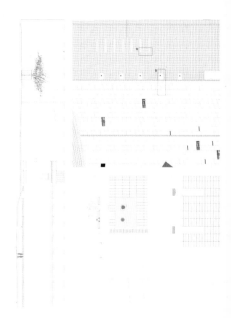

HUD PLAZA IMPROVEMENTS

Architect: Martha Schwartz, Inc.
Location: Washington, D.C., USA
Year: 1998
Sqm: 5 572

Although Marcel Breuer's 1968 building for the Department of Housing and Urban Development (HUD) in Washington, D.C. bears a richly textured facade, its 6-acre plaza is clearly a casualty of the Modernist aesthetic. Without trees or public amenities, the plaza was designed to showcase the building but is virtually unusable by HUD's 4,800 employees. Adding to the desolation of this landscape is the fact that the base of the building is a solid wall of dark stone that prohibits a visual connection between the life of the building within and the outside. HUD's objective for the plaza was to reactivate it by commissioning a new design that would also express the agency's mission of creating habitable spaces for people.

The scheme developed for the plaza repeats a circular motif in white, yellow and grey recalling Breuer's use of geometric designs for screens, walls and ceilings. The plaza is transformed through a strong ground plane, a series of concrete planters containing grass and white lifesaver-shaped canopies. The 30-foot diameter planters double as seating. The canopies, fabricated of vinyl coated plastic fabric, are raised 14 feet above the ground plane on steel poles. In sharp contrast to the heaviness and sombreness of the architecture, these canopies and planters appear to float. As this plaza is built over an underground garage, the canopies also provide shade on a plaza that was not designed to support the soil required for trees.

Lighting gives identity to the plaza as well. Lit from within, the canopies glow at night, recalling the lanterns that illuminate paths in Japanese gardens. A fiber-optic tube casts coloured light under the planters making them appear to float on a cloud of light. For the dark wall at the base of the building, a backlit mural has been planned to reflect the people and faces of HUD and create a dramatic backdrop for the plaza.

LANDSCAPES
AND BRIDGES

Urban settings are not the sole benefactors of artificial illumination. The qualities of natural spaces, such as parks and gardens, can also be enhanced thanks to attractive lighting. The principal reason for planning an illumination project for these kinds of places is the possibility of using them during those hours when natural light is not enough.

It is advisable to approach this type of lighting project with sensitivity towards the landscape, taking into consideration the aesthetic and emotional effect that is desired for each space. A merely functional and homogenous illumination is less attractive than one with a clearer intention that is specifically designed to enhance certain characteristics of the garden. It is preferable to plan the project as a succession of interconnected places, each with their own personality.

The lighting of natural spaces is in general a good occasion to apply the "less is more" principal. Whether the space is a public park or a private garden, there is nothing as distasteful as an exterior space illuminated overzealously in the style of a prison courtyard. The choice of the type of lighting, its position, type of light sources, and the intensity and tones of light are all factors to be carefully analysed.

The safety of the electrical installation is definitely a matter of great importance. The cables and other components should be waterproof, durable, designed for the outdoors, and able to withstand bad weather conditions, extreme temperature changes and corrosive atmospheres, particularly in industrial or coastal settings. The exterior light fittings should be kept free from leaves and organic waste. The electrical installations in these places can be of mains-voltage, 220 volts in continental Europe, or of low voltage; however, a combination of both is also possible. Each option has its pros and cons. In the case of mains-voltage, cables must be specially protected inside semi-elastic plastic tubes and buried at a depth of no less than 50cm (which would be increased if there were any danger of it being uncovered). In the case of low voltage, a transformer modifies the power of the current, so it is less dangerous for children and pets playing nearby. This kind of electric supply is common in domestic settings and private gardens. The selection of the type of transformer will determine how many lights can be positioned in the garden. The exterior plug sockets and light switches should be covered and able to withstand humidity and water.

In private gardens, it is advisable to differentiate between decorative illumination and that of footpaths and security. The latter requires only minimal lighting to ensure safe movement in the hours of darkness, for example, from the street railings to the entrance door of the house. Creating independent lighting systems usually results in substantial energy savings. The footpath lighting could, for example, be activated at night, using heat or movement sensors so that lights shine only when necessary, or when someone walks through the garden.

When planning the lighting scheme of a garden, it is essential to focus on the ambience, character and practical use of the different spaces that form it. It is interesting to create diverse atmospheres in parks and gardens that will suit different moods and sensations. For the exterior, a very subtle illumination is advisable, with brighter pools of light in some zones, such as the dining or barbeque areas. It is also interesting to play with the colour temperature of lighting, using warm and cooler lights to compose contrasted scenes. An economical and effective installation free option is an illumination using candles and fire torches. These elements should be carefully positioned and protected to avoid the risk of fire, especially during the summer months.

A pleasantly lit garden can help expand an interior space. When the exterior lacks illumination, the windows reflect the interior, resulting in the so-called "black mirror" effect. This creates an effect that makes the rooms seem smaller than they really are. It is preferable to achieve a light balance between both sides of the windows so that transparency is also maintained and visually enhanced at night time.

The illumination of ponds and swimming pools makes for another attractive lighting idea. The peripheral lighting of these elements, for example using spotlights fitted into the walls, creates a light of blue and aquatic reflections. It goes without saying that all the lights used in this setting should be waterproof. Water is an extremely reflective element which means an illuminated swimming pool can bring sufficient light to the surrounding areas.

The lighting of exterior garden areas, as with interior and stage illumination, also has its own techniques and resources and the final choice will depend on whatever effect is needed. Up lighting involves illuminating from the bottom upwards. It can create dramatic scenes in the lower areas of trees and greenery. This kind of lighting enhances the size and the presence of the trees and is often done by fitting spotlights into the pavement. Down light illumination is created by street lamps and direct lighting fitted onto the facades of buildings.

It is an efficient system of lighting, albeit rather dull, which does not produce light contamination and is suitable for areas where night time activities take place. Combined with other types of illumination it can help reduce hard shadows produced by certain light sources.

Spot lighting enables certain points in the area to be enhanced thus capturing the attention of the observer. It is ideal to illuminate elements which are worthy of special interest, such as sculptures, water fountains, or plants. In this case, the lights are usually hidden from sight and adjustable.

Another fairly common concept in the illumination of gardens is the positioning of greenery against the light by illuminating a surface: for example, a wall behind the foliage. The silhouettes of the trees are thus highlighted in front of the luminous background. The back wall can be illuminated using waterproof wall-washers.

All these techniques can also be applied to public parks and gardens. The design and cost of illumination in the creation of public spaces and gardens is an essential part of the project. The efficiency of the light sources is paramount and thus many exterior parks and spaces are illuminated with LEDs or photovoltaic elements which use solar energy accumulated during the day. In these places, it is necessary to plan for a minimum level of illumination along the walkways to strengthen safety. It is advisable to illuminate paths and walkways in parks at ground level with dimmed lighting thus creating relaxing ambiences free from dazzling. When the lights located in the garden cannot be concealed, they should be discrete and enhance the mysterious effect of nature illuminated by artificial light.

LANDSCAPES

The image of a place can change radically at night-time. Darkness can render a peaceful field into a disturbing and gloomy place. The artificial lighting of a landscape can be proposed in many different situations, in both urban and natural settings. Parks, large public spaces in trade fairs or diverse events, natural spaces close to the city with varying degrees of human input, zones of indefinite use on the outskirts and so on are just some examples of cases in which the illumination of landscapes is considered.

The strategies used to plan this type of illumination are also very diverse. One is to imitate nature - for example by recreating the light of a full moon. The "moon-lighting" technique involves just that - a soft descending illumination in blue tones at very low levels of intensity (approx. 0.2 lux of light).

Another strategy is to build a landscape using the light, colours and strips of light which touch on the principals of land art. Although there are many technical, ecological and maintenance aspects to be considered in these types of illumination projects, their real "raison d'être" is to provoke emotion and aesthetic pleasure in those who contemplate them at night.

BRANDGRENS ROTTERDAM
THE FIRE LIMITS

Architect: West 8 urban design & landscape architecture b.v.

Location: Rotterdam, The Netherlands

Year: 2007

Surface: 12 km

West 8's design uses light objects to mark the fire limits. An iconic image of a flame is incorporated in circular light objects on the ground and in several information stations, that together form the marking.

The image of the flame shows a visual connection with Zadkine's statue commemorating the bombing of Rotterdam.

The light objects come to life at night when the solar-powered LEDs illuminate the icon. This physical marking of the fire limits is coupled with information about the historic meaning of the bombing, accessible through the information stations and a website.

LANDSCAPES

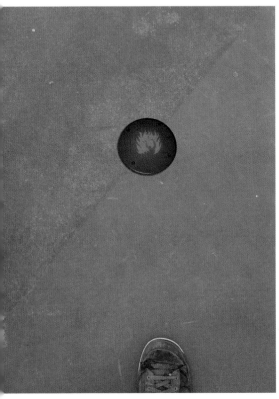

METROPOL PARASOL

Architect: J. Mayer H. Architects
Location: Seville, Spain
Year: under construction - 2009
Sqm: 5 000

Metropol Parasol is the new iconic project for Seville. It explores the potential of the Plaza de la Encarnación to become the new contemporary urban centre. Its role as a unique urban space within the dense fabric of the medieval inner city of Seville allows for a great variety of activities such as contemplation, leisure and commerce. A highly developed infrastructure helps to activate the square, making it an attractive destination for tourists and locals alike.

The Metropol Parasol scheme with its large mushroom-like structures offers an archeological site, a farmers market, an elevated plaza, multiple bars and restaurants underneath and inside the parasols, as well as a panoramic terrace on the very top of the parasols. Thought of as a light wood structure, the parasols grow out of the archeological excavation site into a contemporary landmark. The columns become prominent points of access to the museum below as well as to the Plaza and panoramic deck above, defining a unique relationship between the historical and the contemporary city.

The Metropolitan Parasol is conceived as a roof structure that provides precious shade during the day, creating a comfortable microclimate and a place for relaxation. At night, the MP becomes an artificial sky that sets the stage for various light and sound scenarios. These two qualities allow for a series of urban activities such as sports (beach volleyball, boxing, street basketball, etc.), cultural events (cinema, theatre, concerts, etc.), as well as commercial uses (car and fashion shows, corporate events, presentations, etc.) that emphazise the Plaza's role as one of the city's main places for communication and interaction.

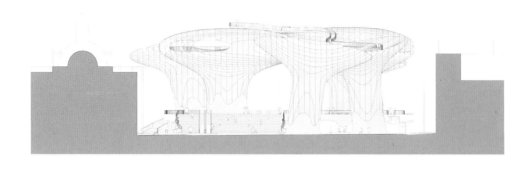

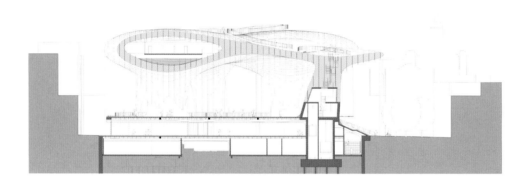

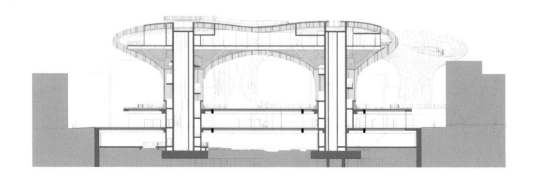

NUIT DES DOCKS

Lighting artist: Yann Kersalé

Location: Saint Nazaire, France

Year: 1991

Joël Batteux, mayor of Saint-Nazaire, commissioned Yann Kersalé to under-take a study on the site of the docks of the town in 1989. The mayor suc-ceeded in getting this installation approved in a township where the inde-structible submarine base has remained a haunting reminder of the war. Refrigerators, grain elevators, elevating gear, mobile cranes, turnbridges, swingbridges and drawbridges are illuminated in a minimalist style accord-ing to their structure by white static lights, except for the submarine-base cells which are blue. The mobile features, cranes and bridges produce lu-minous pulsations when set in movement. All structures are equipped with a small red light on the port side, green on the starboard side, echoing the light beacons that indicate the entrance to the harbour.

When the decision-makers saw the site all lit up, they realised the full value and the beauty of their industrial heritage. The roads were tarred, hangars repaired, paint-work refreshed. A work of art destined for a public space must be able to resist all possible aggression. The competition open for the development and maintenance of the installations followed the schedule of the conditions completely, and the choice of the materials turned out to be perfect.

Later, the town council took over the follow-up for the maintenance work, and every night a technical service officer carries out security checks. This work, which has reconciled Saint-Nazaire with its port, has become an extra-ordinary public relations tool, as proof that art can have a profound influ-ence on a town, and not necessarily in merely a place dedicated to it.

Nuit des Docks has contributed to Saint-Nazaire's renaissance through the fact that the town has renewed its connection with its harbour.

L'Ô QUAI BRANLY MUSEUM

Architect: Jean Nouvel

Lighting artist: Yann Kersalé

Location: Paris, France

Year: 2006

Sqm: 17 000

Once the sun sets and the museum's garden shuts down, one's eyesight travels across the glass palisade, above the ditches of the rue de l'Université. In the midst of the garden, a water-like glow embraces the tall grass. This aquatic light intensifies as the night falls. Where yesterday it was a greenish blue, palpitating similar to a field of lavender, it is today nearly white underneath the winter. This urban and nocturnal lake consists of thousands of luminous stems planted within the vegetation. The stems have the ability to change colour whenever a digital thermometer commands them to do so. Within this garden, the shades range from opaque green to bluish white in relation to the weather. The heat creates a water mist which makes the lake of light appear a fresh shade of green in the Parisian night. In winter, when the water's temperature drops near zero, a bluish white glow appears and so lives the lake of light with rhythms reflected by the foliage.

L'Ô is an artistic intervention by Yann Kersalé for the Quai Branly Museum. Yann Kersalé has imagined a light piece which goes along with Jean Nouvel's architecture for exteriors, and has collaborated with the landscape designer Gilles Clément in the garden. In the garden, Yann proposes a lake of light which brings vegetation to life underneath the museum. Thousands of luminous rushes change in colour according to the meteorological movements, ranging from blue to green, coming back to white all through the night and throughout the year along with the vegetation's lifespan. As the plants gradually grow, the rushes will eventually be more or less covered up, thus creating a unique atmosphere.

This lake of light is made possible by the 'plantation' of over 1200 rushes ranging from 30 cm to 2 meters high, controlled by a box linked to a meteorological station.

ERCO LICHTWIESE

Lighting Planning: Belzner Holmes
Location: Lüdenscheid, Germany
Year: 2001
Sqm: 25 000

With the onset of dusk the premises of ERCO Leuchten GmbH becomes a "Lichtwiese" (German, "light-meadow"). On the way through the premises the visitor enters a fascinating light-world. Through dramatic staging the visitor is taken from scene to scene and from mood to mood. In this way ERCO shows the possibilities that outdoor lighting offers.

On buildings and premises ERCO displays typical concepts like the illumination of facades and paths, and details on buildings, trees and shrubs. Based on this unique lighting, effects are shown for special occasions. Changing scenarios and lighting sequences are controlled by ERCO's Lightcontrol device and are used through remote control. The differentiated light qualities are achieved through the properties of the different luminaries, lamps, light directions and light colours.

On the approximately 25,000 sqm park-like premises more than 150 luminaries have been installed by lighting architects Belzner-Holmes, Heidelberg. Here the lighting manufacturer is testing the new outdoor luminaries concerning their effect and presents the possibilities of their use. Therefore the "Lichtwiese" corresponds to mock-up spaces for interior lighting.

BRIDGES

Given their gravity defying characteristics, bridges are elements of great expression and strength. Their illumination, as well as facilitating the walk across a space, enables them to be contemplated at night time. Bridges such as those in Brooklyn, New York and those that cross the Seine in Paris are unforgettable sights of these cities. Also, the numerous walkways over the canals of cities such as Venice and Amsterdam are without question charming places bursting with romanticism where their magic is enhanced by the appropriate lighting.

The illumination of a bridge, as with that of any technical structure or artistic object, should endeavour to highlight the most interesting elements of the engineering feature. For example, the illumination of the Millau Bridge, designed by the architect Norman Foster, brings out its light and lineal aspect as it appears to float above the hills. In the case of the Millenium Bridge in London, built by Wilkinson Eyre Architects, the sinuous curves of the structure create a dynamic effect. Sometimes illumination is planned to vary according to the time of day, such as that designed by James Turrell and l'Observatoire International for the Pont du Gard. In this case, light varies constantly, sometimes highlighting the arches and the material character of the stone of this old bridge and at other times minimizing its presence with blue light that matches the nocturnal skies.

SACKLER CROSSING BRIDGE

Architect: John Pawson

Location: Royal Botanic Gardens, Kew, UK

Year: 2006

In 2004 the decision was made to commission what is the latest in a series of architectural interventions at Royal Botanic Gardens, Kew – a bridge across the lake.

Following Capability Brown's preference for the 'sinuous Line of Grace,' the bridge plots a serpentine path across the water. The deck is set the minimum possible distance from the lake's surface, allowing those crossing to feel that they are literally taking a walk across the water. This sense of proximity is enhanced by glimpsed views of the lake between the deck treads and by the near invisibility of the supporting structures which lends the bridge a quality of sculptural abstraction. Clear visual connections are established between the manmade landscape of the bridge and the repeating natural forms of its setting: the gently rounded contours of the land, the smooth expanse of water and the powerful verticals of the trees.

A spare material palette of granite and bronze reinforces the elemental character of the design. Rhythmic bands of dark granite laid like railway sleepers form the deck, while cast bronze vertical cantilevers set flush between the granite treads act as simple balusters, the top of each slender upright smoothly contoured to fit comfortably in the hand. Viewed end on, the balusters read as a solid composition. From the side this solidity fragments, allowing views through and affording the structure a pleasing material ambiguity, with light used to preserve this transparency after nightfall.

The 120-hectare expanse of Kew's Royal Botanic Gardens lies south-west of London. Set in a curve of the Thames River, its tranquillity untouched by the incongruous proximity of planes making their final descent into Heathrow, this is a rich palimpsest of landscape and iconic structures shaped by the work of the leading designers of their day, including Capability Brown and Decimus Burton.

MARSUPIAL BRIDGE AND URBAN PLAZA

Architect: La Dallman Architects
Location: Milwaukee, Wisconsin, USA
Year: 2006

The intent of this multi-phased project was to revitalise the zone surrounding the Milwaukee River's 1925 Holton Street Viaduct. The project consists of interwoven components: a 'Marsupial' Bridge that hangs beneath the viaduct, offering a new pedestrian and bicycle connection which joins both sides of the river, and an Urban Plaza also under the viaduct, acting as a civic space and media garden. Because the location beneath the viaduct inherently lacks natural daylight, the project's success relied on innovative and sensitive illumination strategies.

As a "green highway," the Marsupial Bridge hangs opportunistically from the over-structured middle third of the viaduct's trolley structure. The Marsupial Bridge's undulate post-tension concrete deck offers a counterpoint to the existing steel members of the viaduct, inspired by the notion of weaving a new spine through the structure. Step lighting is integrated linearly behind the apron and through the wood rail. This lighting system is augmented by precision theatrical fixtures (framing projectors) that are mounted above to create a focused ribbon of illumination with minimal spill into the riparian topography.

The Urban Plaza (aka Media Garden / village green) converts an unsafe, barren underbridge area into a civic gathering space for film festivals, regattas and other river events. The internally illuminated benches provide a respite for pedestrians and bicyclists as they make their way across the Marsupial Bridge. By night, the glowing concrete benches serve as functional art forms, transforming the Plaza into a welcoming and mysterious moonscape for the neighbourhood.

This open space strategy challenges the traditional notion of public space as a "town square," or "village green," a
provides a site-specific solution for the underbridge zone.

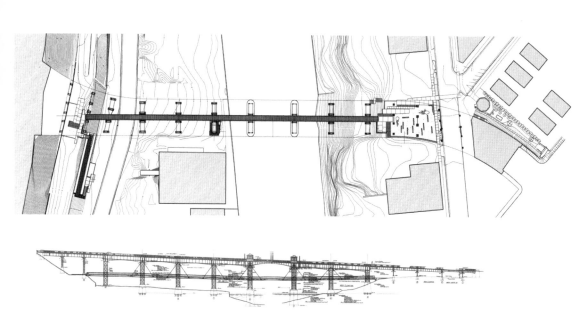

GATESHEAD MILLENNIUM BRIDGE

Architect: Wilkinson Eyre

Location: Gateshead, UK

Year: 2001

Winner of the 2002 RIBA Stirling Prize, this unique crossing for pedestrians and cyclists has already become a new landmark for Gateshead and the Tyne, a river famous for its historic bridges. The opening motion of the design is both its generator and its highlight transforming the static sculptural form in a theatrical kinetic event.

The idea is simple; a pair of arches, one forming the deck, the other supporting it, pivots around their common springing point to allow ships to pass beneath. The motion is efficient and rational, yet dramatic beyond the capabilities of previously explored opening mechanisms. The whole bridge tilts, and as it does the composition undergoes a metamorphosis into a 'grand arch' of great width and grace, in an operation which evokes the action of a closed eye slowly opening.

The scheme is wholly informed by the need for a legible integration with the Tyne's existing bridges and with its particular context. The design is a mix of the robust, as befits its lineage, combined with an overall lightness to contrast the visual mass of the Baltic Flour Mill. A soaring arch provides instant visual reference to the Tyne Bridge beyond but presents a slender profile against the skyline, interpreting and updating the structural and aesthetic order of its neighbour.

The bridge spans between new islands running parallel to the quay sides. Public access to these caissons offers exciting additions to the functions of the bridge, allowing a glazed hall on each to provide amenities in a highly dramatic location with incredible views of the structure and the Tyne. The bridge between these two caissons features two parallel decks separated by level and intermittent screening to differentiate pedestrian and cycle paths.

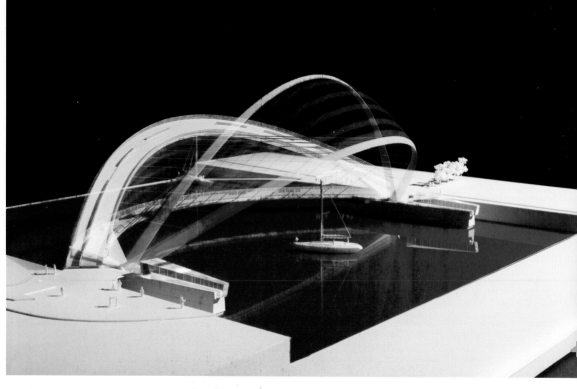

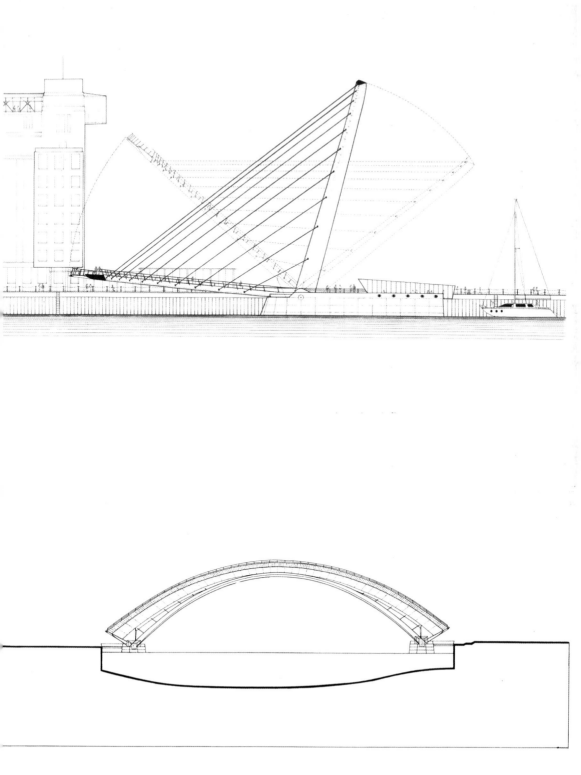

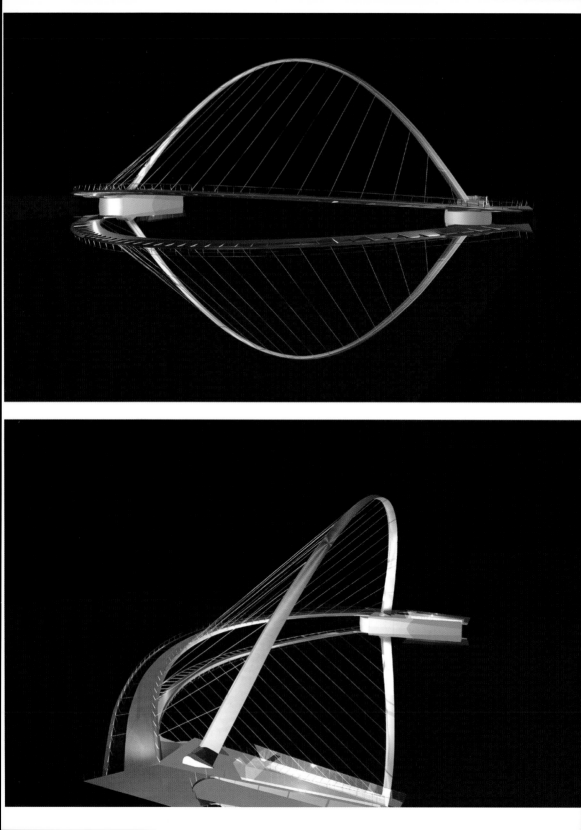

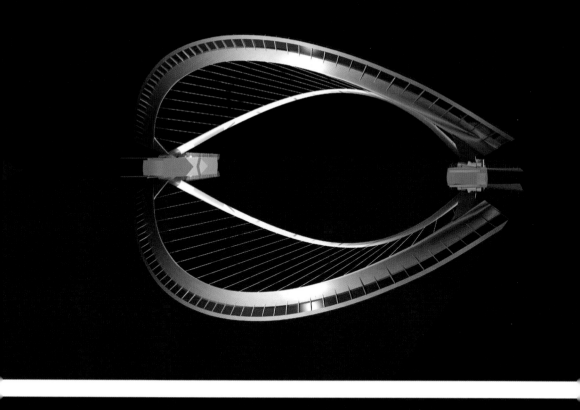

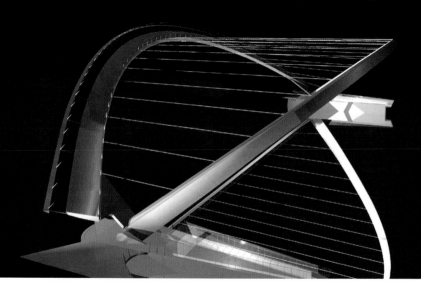

MEMORIALS AND EVENTS

The illumination designed for temporary exhibitions and events and for the contemplation of commemorative monuments strives to provoke sensations which in some way move the observer. This makes it one of the fields with the greatest levels of artistic ambition and permits a higher degree of experimentation. Often, lighting effects which have worked well in temporary exhibitions or events are subsequently applied to buildings and urban spaces using new techniques. Art and technology are closely related so that advances in lighting material and installations and the ideas of artists or lighting specialists draw inspiration from each other.

There are really no intrinsic characteristics in regards to temporary lighting installations. Generally they allow a greater level of freedom and daring; however their budgets are usually more limited depending on each individual project. Contracting the services of a lighting specialist to give an event an extra touch of brightness or to catch the attention of potential clients in trade fairs or exhibitions is increasingly common. A clear example is the installation for Moët & Chandon, designed by PTW Architects, in Melbourne, Australia, which took place in November 2005. It consisted of a 10 x 10 meter white space illuminated by soft daylight flowing through a tensioned Lycra textile which had been digitally patterned and custom-tailored for the space. The resulting ambience was relaxing and futuristic. Another temporary stand worth mentioning is the Mitsubishi Motor Showroom (2002) designed by the Japanese architect Jun Aoki. This commercial installation plays with specular reflections so that a crumpled stainless steel sheet creates deformed images of the cars on show. At other times, it is the design of a temporary (or permanent) exhibition in a museum or gallery which requires this kind of intervention. A fine example of this is "The city of K. Franz Kafka and Prague" by curator Juan Insúa presented in the CCCB, Barcelona in 1999, which combined the concept of the illumination and the subject of the exhibit itself with great sensitivity and interest. Shadows, half-light and mirrors are used to immerse the visitors in the mysterious and disturbing world of the author's novels.

Today, many lighting projects for commemorative monuments and sculptures begin with an aesthetical approach, which doesn't mean all other practical matters can be forgotten. This area of work is becoming evermore sophisticated and ambitious. It is much more complex than spotlighting the object with lamps. The aim of lighting is to provoke a lasting memory or an emotion which leads the observer to some kind of thought related to the subject of the monument. A prime example is the monument commemorating the victims of 11-M in the Atocha train station in Madrid, designed by the architect studio F.A.M. With the concept of creating a "bluish void," light reaches the interior through a glass cylinder, on which the names of the victims of the terrorist attack are screen-printed.

Light has a decisive effect on monuments and sculptures and should, as in the case of architectural lighting, support and favour the artistic concept which is apparent in the piece. A good example is the illumination designed by Hervé Descottes and l'Observatoire International for the reproduction of Brancusi's slender Endless column, in the park of the same name in Targu-Jiu, in Romania. During the day the point where the column ends is easily visible.

Somehow, reality betrays the artist's idea and the observer can make out the end of the column. At night, the artificial illumination assumes a softer tone as the light slowly rises up the tower.

Exactly as Brancusi must have imagined, the column seems to disappear into the darkness of the night sky, appearing finally, endless. The monument commemorates the soldiers who lost their lives in the First World War. It appears to show the way up to heaven for the souls who fell in combat.

The illumination of sculptures deserves a profound understanding of the concepts and aesthetic values which the artwork wishes to convey. Some of the projects of the lighting specialist Joost van Santen demonstrate interesting interactions between the objects being illuminated, the surrounding space and the artificial light. This can be seen in the sculpture of the head quarters of ING Bank where reflections, shadows, and brighter areas become indissoluble components of the artwork. The perception of the observer is considered thoroughly by contemplating all aspects which may affect the view of the space. In another of his projects, the Palace of Justice of The Hague, Joost van Santen has created an innovative element based on the decomposition of white light into the distinct colours of the visible spectrum. The dull and rational aspect of the building alters dramatically due to the fun and clever use of oblique light and holographic reflectors which colour the space.

Traditionally, other urban elements such as fountains and water jets have been illuminated in towns. A classic, yet attractive example can be seen in Barcelona, in the choreographies of light, water and music of the Montjuic Fountain, designed by the Catalan engineer Carlos Buigas. The combination of water and light produces fascinating and eye-catching effects. Another outstanding example is the Crown Fountain, by the artist Jaume Plensa in the Millenium Park in Chicago. It consists of two tall glass brick towers above a sheet of water. Images of human faces are projected onto the two opposite towers. At times, real water shoots out of their virtual mouths, refreshing the ambience of the square.

A large number of contemporary artists investigate the possibilities of manipulating and conditioning our vision of exterior reality by using light. In some ways their "perception laboratories" are subsequently applied to architecture and interior design in very different circumstances. For example, LED billboards with moving written messages, truly characteristic of the American artist Jenny Holzer, have later been used by architects like Herzog & de Meuron and Jean Nouvel in some of their proposals. Two fine examples are the project for the Cultural Centre of Blois and the new facade of the Jussieu Library in Paris – both projected by the Swiss architects. Regarding the work of Holzer, she endeavours to criticise the appropriation of urban space and its commercialization by businesses and advertisers. The artists Nic Hess and Manfred Erjautz agree on this subject with their luminous reproductions of advertising logos.

On other occasions the inspiration for light installations comes from nature itself. In the work Your Intuitive Sky (2000), the artist Olafur Eliasson creates a sky with clouds which float across in front of the sun. Several works of the Scandinavian Thorbjörn Lausten artificially reproduce the colours of an aurora borealis in areas close to the North Pole. In the temporary exhibition Fiber (2004), held at the National Museum of Emerging Science and Innovation in Japan, the architect Jun Aoki converts the interior space into a rainy and stormy night. The lighting design transforms a series of fibre thread curtains into an intense downpour. The evolution of illumination techniques along with the sensitivity of artists and designers enables the creation of truly beautiful images.

MEMORIALS

Aside from the technical and safety requirements, there are no set norms in the illumination of urban sculptures and monuments. Sensitivity and conceptual clarity is perhaps a good base from which to start. Simplicity in the lighting design of certain commemorative monuments is more effective than over-complicating the set up.

A moving example is the simplicity of the Vietnam War Memorial in Washington D.C., created by Maya Lin, which consists of a black stone wall where the names of the American victims have been inscribed and softly illuminated by lights fitted into the pavement.

MONUMENT COMMEMORATING
THE VICTIMS OF MARCH 11, 2004

Architect: Estudio FAM
Location: Madrid
Year: 2007
Sqm: 500

The project is presented for tender using the theme: light dedicates a moment of the day to each person no longer with us. The report of tender continues two years later, explaining the intentions of the project in depth.

"The monument rises up from the depths of the RENFE station – from the scene of pain itself, and as a cry of hope that wants to be seen by the city of Madrid. The Project embodies an inaccesible place which is contemplated from the open city and the silence of the interior of the station. The monument, as regards its relationship with the exterior, portrays the strength of the moment trapped for eternity."

The monument consists of two closely related parts, which only together make sense - the work carried out on the interior room in order to view the dome created by the messages and the glass structure itself which brings the whole idea to life.

The glass sculpture involves two different parts - the exterior compressed monolithic glass skin and the transparent interior membrane which holds the messages. Given its use, the exterior glass must be totally colourless and of great purity to allow the view of the vacuum from the interior room of the station. The space of the representation contains a dark space where light flows in through the perforations in the wrought iron to illuminate the interior and an interior covered by a veil of blue light. The room is acoustically isolated to enhance the silence and respect that the monument deserves. It is a free open space filled by light.

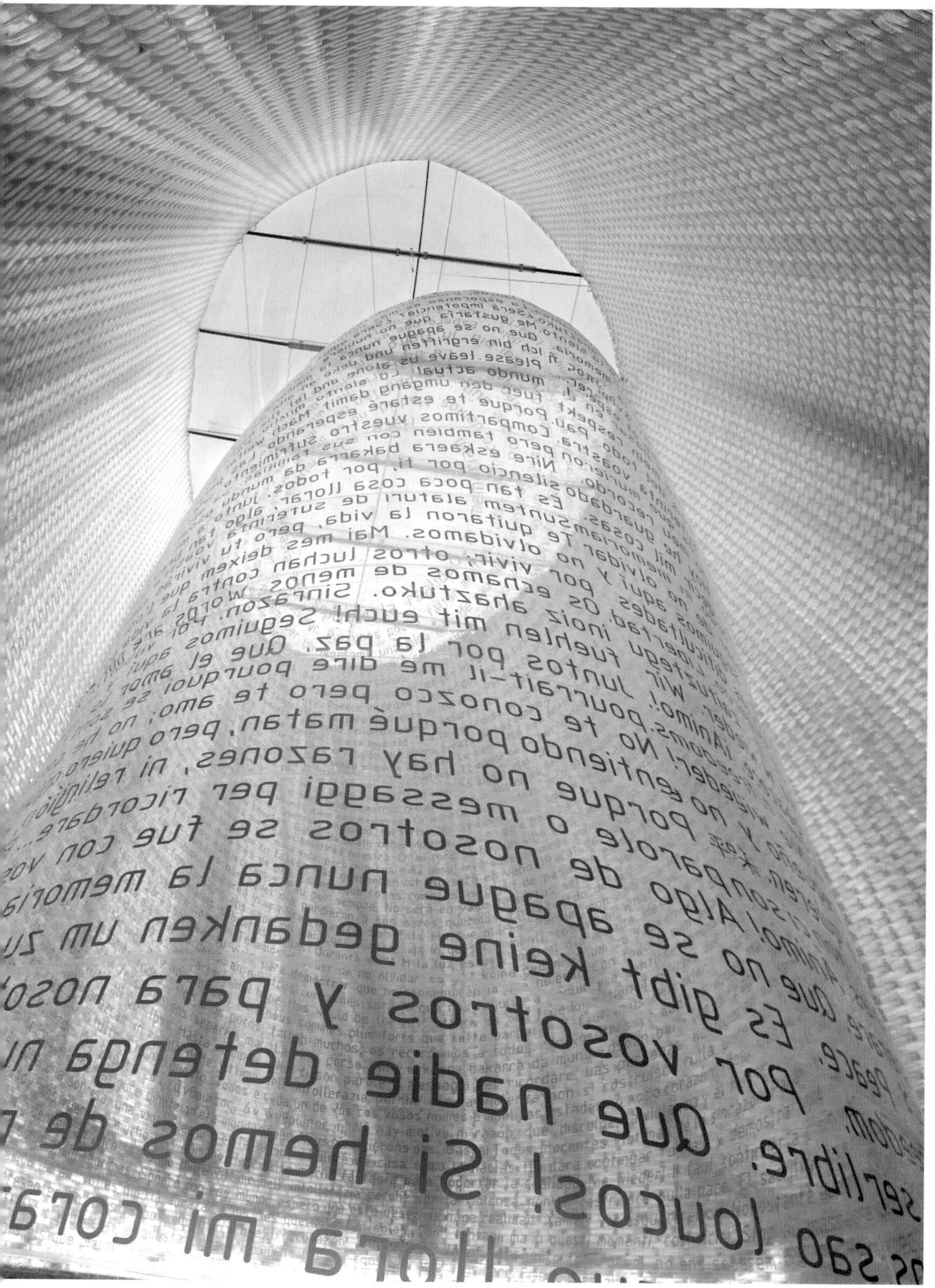

MEMORIALS

LOUVRE

Architect: Rudy Ricciotti and Mario Bellini
Location: Paris, France
Year: 2005
Sqm: 5 000

Mario Bellini and Rudy Ricciotti have searched for the "friendly and non-violent integration" of a contemporary architectural project within an historic building. The presented collections are distributed throughout 3500 sqm on two levels, the ground floor and basement presenting the works from the 7th to the 9th century, including the prestigious collection of carpets.

The natural light is spread out like a many-layered veil which serves to focus the light's intensity and avoid glare. In the summertime, the intense lighting of the interior of the space does not exceed the recommended levels for the conservation of the artwork and the comfort of the visitors.

In the basement, the veil of light is present in numerous places because of strategic openings, conserving the veil as a unifying role in the collection. It creates a subtle mosaic effect in which the light adds profundity and beauty.

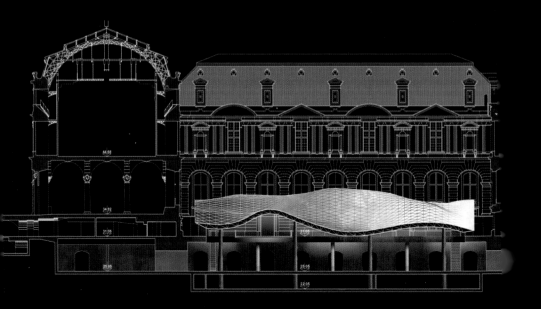

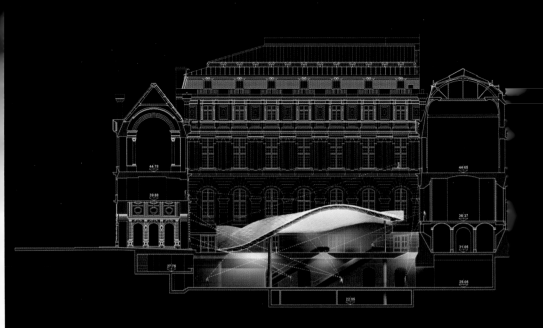

EVENTS

Many factors have contributed to illumination being increasingly important in temporary installations and events. The evolution of light technology, greater efficiency of light sources and their ever growing variety and chromatic quality encourages greater creativity in such projects.

Certain institutions and local authorities are realising the benefits this can bring. For example, since 2000, the French town of Bourges now celebrates during the summer months, "Nuits Lumières", which involves the careful and avant-garde illumination of the old part of town. The result is simply unforgettable. In Paris and Berlin there have also been very attractive lighting displays, such as the temporary illumination of the Canal de Saint Martin in Paris created by the specialist Yann Kersalé and some of the projects by the realities:united collective in Berlin.

A BLANC NUIT BLANCHE

Lighting artist: Yann Kersalé
Location: Canal Saint Martin, Paris, France
Year: 2003

In the event of the Parisian Nuit Blanche, in 2003, 110 sites in Paris were placed in the hands of visitors by night. Yann Kersalé was asked to create a temporary lighting installation for the St. Martin Canal, under the artistic direction of Gérard Paque.

It was set up from the La Villette pool to the Temple navigation lock. The principle was to illuminate the canal with a white, cold and extremely luminous light, where the light would reveal the hidden appearance of the landscape and architecture, invisible in daylight.

"One can dream that one day the nights of the St. Martin Canal become a sort of map of the sensitive sparse sensations following a visionary treasure hunt. A mysterious and seductive promenade from the Seine to the Seine. The canal from one end to another, a transversal from suburbia to Paris and from Paris to suburbia. A whole fragmented by the overexposure of multi-shaped objects that build it."

The actual proposal is to pick certain objects and accentuate them in the context of the surrounding urban light, with a very white, near silver, light.

MOET MARQUEE
ESPACE LUMIERE

Architect: PTW Architects, Chris Bosse
Location: Melbourne, Australia
Year: 2005
Sqm: 100

PTW architects together with Amanda Henderson from Gloss Creative designed the Moët & Chandon Marquee for the Melbourne Cup 2005, the biggest annual horse racing event in Australia. The architects used the latest digital technologies from concept-sketch to realisation to create a sparkling and surreal atmosphere in the name of the "Bubble-ism."

Through the use of daylight and a tensioned Taiyo-Lycra material that is digitally patterned and custom-tailored for the space, a 10x10 "off the shelf" marquee was transformed into a space that the press describes as an "avant-garde environment not of this earth."

The project renounces the application of a structure in the traditional sense. Instead, the space is filled with a three-dimensional lightweight sculpture, solely based on minimal surface tension, freely stretching between wall and ceiling and floor.

The lightweight fabric construction of the pavilion follows the lines and surface tension of soap films, stretching between ground and sky. These natural curves of bubbles are translated into an organic three-dimensional space.

By partially letting sunlight penetrate "through" the fabric structure, the pavilion comes to life as an ephemeral and surreal bubble experience. The perforated ceiling filters natural light and directs it onto and through the Lycra fabric, creating the depth and translucency of the space, the ephemeral quality. The light changes constantly during the day with moving clouds and changing atmospheric conditions.

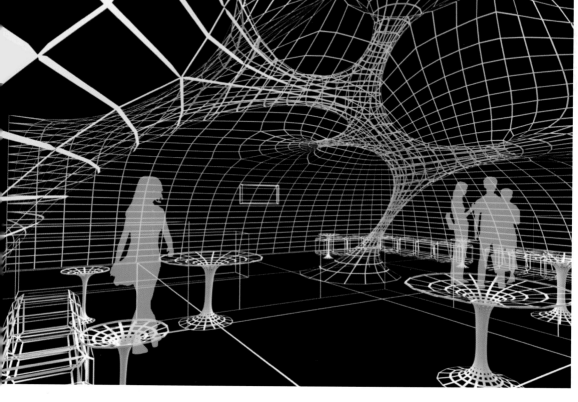

EVENTS

ROADSHOW PHILIPS: COLONSCOPE

Architect: Francisco Mangado
Architectural Lighting Solution: Antón Amann
Location: Itinerant
Year: 2005
Sqm: 14,8

In the production of an itinerant and ephemeral architecture, conditioned in its dimensions as an industrial "container," another opportunity to reflect on the transforming capacity of architecture and its condition as transmitter of specific sensations is given. It also provides a real life scenario where the possibilities of the use of light/illumination as an architectural instrument can be explored, as can the way it is used in transforming spaces, and the enhancing or filtering of these sensations.

The container is converted into an abstract tunnel space which evokes the primitive cave with the construction of an interior covering of simple laminate elements perpendicularly laid out on the walls themselves. The whole vision in perspective reconstructs a faceted surface of complex geometry and reminiscent of mineral environments.

The construction of this scenic succession of "frames" gives the space an intense sensation of fluidity and movement which is enhanced by the use of digitally synchronised dynamic sound and lighting. The idea is to remove the visitor from the "fairground" setting which these events portray and submerge him or her in the architectural experience proposed by lessening the real chromatic vision inside the container using highly pure monochromatic light produced by blue LED lamps. In this decontextualising effort the abstract and enveloping sound which supports this illuminated architecture will play a crucial role.

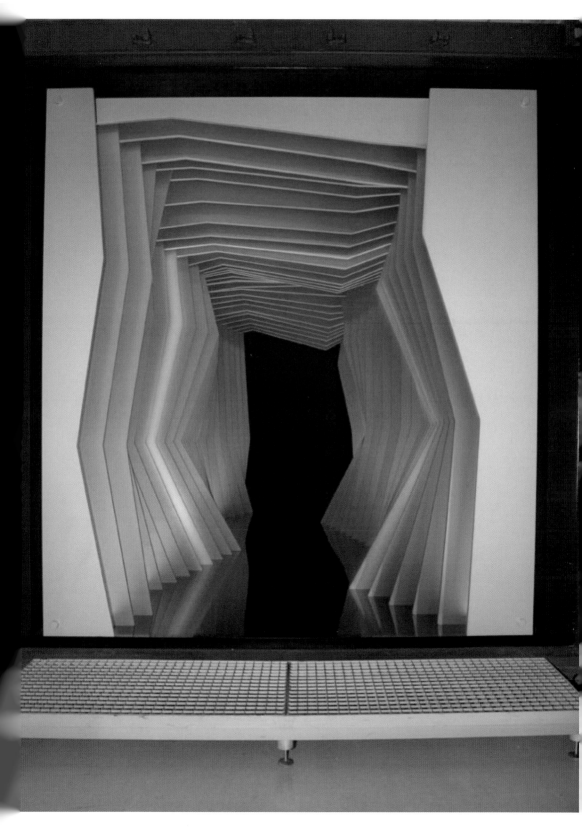

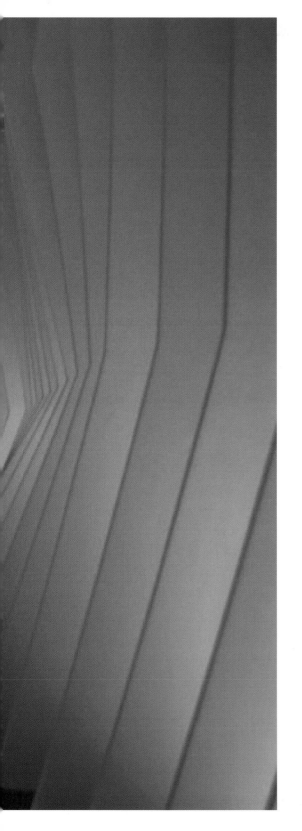

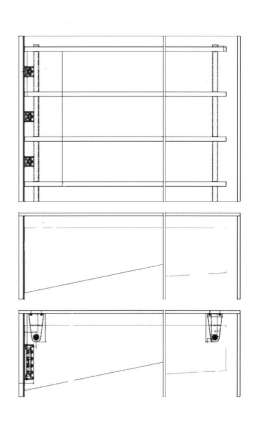

Aires Mateus
www.airesmateus.com
Centro de Artes de Sines
Photos: © Aires Mateus

Ag4 media facade Gmbh
www.ag4.de
Media Facade T-Mobile
Photos: ©ag4 media facade Gmbh

Alles Wird Gut, Wein
www.alleswirdgut.cc/awg.php
Si Einfamilienhaus
Photos: © Alles Wird Gut

Asymptote
www.asymptote.net
HydraPier
Photos: © Christian Richters

Alsop
www.alsoparchitects.com
The Blizard Building
Photos: © Alsop Design

Andrés Jaque Arquitectos
www.andresjaque.net
Casa Sacerdotal Diocesana de Plasencia
Photos: © Miguel de Guzman

Belzner Holmes
www.belznerholmes.de
Erco P3
Erco LIchtwiese
Photos: © Belzner Holmes
Lighting Design Marstall Mensa
Photos: © Thomas Ott, Darmstadt

Bernard Tschumi Architects
www.tschumi.com
Limoges Concert Hall
Alfred Lerner Hall Student Center
Flon Railway and Bus Station
Photos: © Bernard Tschumi Architects

Camenzind Grafensteiner Architects
www.camenzindgrafensteiner.com
Tyre Shop - Art Exchange
Photos: © Martina Issler, Peter Würmli

David Adjaye
www.adjaye.com
Art Pavilion
Whitechapel Idea Store
Nobel Peace Center
Photos: © Adjaye Associates

Edge Design
www.edge.hk.com
Broadway Cineplex
Photos: © Edge Design

Eldrige Smerin Architects
www.eldridgesmerin.com
House in Highgate
Villa Moda
Bt Cellmet '02 Mobile Applications
Photos: © Eldridge Smerin

Estudio Barozzi Veiga
www.barozziveiga.com
Consejo Regulador Ribera O.Duero
Photos: © Estudio Barozzi Veiga

Estudio FAM
www.estudiofam.co
Commemorative Monument in memory
of the victims of March 11 2004
Photos: © Estudio FAM

Foster and Partners
www.fosterandpartners.com
Free University
Photos: © Foster and Partners

Francisco José Mangado Beloqui
www.fmangado.com
Paris Offices
Auditorio y Palacio de Congresos
de Navarra
Roadshow Philips Colonoscope
Photos: © Mangado y Asociados
Dalí Square
Photos: © Miguel de Guzmán
Pey Berland square
Photos: © C.Desile

GMG Architekten
www.gmg-architekten.de
The Christ Pavilion Expo 2000 and
Volkenroda Monastery
Photos: © GMG Archikten

Jean Nouvel
www.jeannouvel.com
Agbar Tower
Photos: © Ateliers Jean Nouvel
Drawings: © Gaston Bergeret

J. Mayer H. Architects
www.jmayerh.de
Stadt.haus
Photos: © David Franck
Metropol Parasol
Photos: © J.Meyer H. Architects

John Pawson
www.johnpawson.com
Sackler Crossing Bridge
Photos: © RBG kew / A.McRobb

Jun Aoki & Associates
www.aokijun.com
Luis Vuitton Omotesando
Photos: © Louis Vuitton / Nacasa
& Partners Inc., Marc Plantec
Louis Vuitton Ginza Namiki
Louis Vuitton Nagoya
Photos: © Stephane Murate,
Louis Vuitton / Jimmy Cohrssen

Jun Aoki & Associates
www.aokijun.com
Aomori Museum of Art
Photos: © Aomori Museum of Art

Jun Itami
www.junitami.com
Three Art Museums
Photos: © Jun Itami

Kuba & Pilar Architeki
www.arch.cz/kuba.pilar/
Department Store Omega
Faculty of Arts, Library,
Masaryk University
Photos: © Kuba &Pilar Architekti

La Dallman Architechts
www.ladallman.com
Marsupial Bridge and Urban Plaza
Photos: © La Dallman Architects

Martha Swartz, Inc., Washington
www.marthaschwartz.com
Hud Plaza Improvements
Photos: © Alan Ward, Don Sharp

Massimiliano Fuksas
http://art.dada.it/fuksas/home.htm
New Trade Fair Milano
Photos: © Archivio Fuksas, Philippe Ruault
Europark 2 Inseln
Photos: © Philippe Ruault

Nieto Sobejano Arquitectos, S.L.
www.nietosobejano.com
Ampliación de la Sede de Kastner Ohler
Espacio de Creación
Artística Contemporanea
Photos: © Nieto Sobejano Architects

Norihiko Dan
www.dan-n.co.jp/topenglish.html
Sado Bottling Factori Nisaco
Photos: © Kozo Takayama,
Norihiko Dan and Associates

Patrick Jouin and l'Observatoire
www.patrickjouin.com
Mix Restaurant
Photos: © Thomas Duval, Eric Laignel

PTW Architects & Chris Bosse
www.ptw.com.au
Möet Marquee, Espace Lumière
Photos: © PTW Architects & Chris Bosse

RCR Arquitectes
www.rcrarquitectes.es
Guarderia Els Colors
Photos: © E.Pons, RCR, H.Suzuki

realities:united
www.realities-united.de
Spots Light
Photos: © 2005/06 Bernd Hiepe, Berlin
Drawings: © 2005 realities:united, Berlin
Bix Project
Photos: © 2003 E. Klamminger, Graz, 2003 Harry Schiffer, Graz, 2003 realities:united, Berlin
Drawings: © 2001-03 realities:united, Berlin
Powerplant Artistic Light Installation
Photos: © Realities United, Berlin

Renzo Piano Building Workshop
www.rpbw.com
Niccolo Paganini Aditorium
Photos: © Renzo Piano Building Workshop

Rudi Ricciotti
www.rudyricciotti.com
National Choreographic Centre in
Aix-en-Provence
Photos: © JC Carbonne
Mucem
Louvre
Photos: ©Rudi Ricciotti

Saia Barbarese Topouzanov Architectes
www.sbt.qc.ca
Palais des Congrés
Photos: © Marc Cramer

Un Studio
www.unstudio.com
Galleria Department Store
Photos: © Un Studio
Cartell Zuoz
Photos: © Un Studio

West 8 Urban Design &
Landscape Architects
www.west8.nl
Brandgrens Rotterdam
Photos: © West8

Wilkinson Eyre
www.wilkinsoneyre.com
Gateshead Millenium Bridge
Photos: © Wilkinson Eyre Architects Limited

Yann Kersalé
www.ykersale.com
In Out Sony Center
L'ô Musée du quai Branly
Nuit des Docks
Nuit Blanche
Photos: © Yann Kersalé

Zaha Hadid
www.zaha-hadid.com
The Taichung Metropolitan Opera House
Elefheria Square
Drawings: © Zaha Hadid